THE MILLENNIUM THOUGHTS
Challenges to Survival

THE MILLENNIUM THOUGHTS
Challenges to Survival

K. Balan

AUTHORSPRESS

First Published 2001
by Authorspress

E-35/103, Jawahar Park (Shree Ganesh Complex),
Laxmi Nagar, Delhi-110 092

e-mail: authorspress@yahoo.com
quantum_soul@mantramail.com

Typeset in NewCenturySchlbk by Chitra Computers

The Millennium Thoughts
ISBN 81-7273-063-2

Printed in India at Tarun Offset, Delhi.

Preface

The third millennium is an era of formidable challenges and problems. The first and foremost challenge is the threat of annihilation. Today, the choice before mankind is self-destruction or survival. The imminent danger is from nuclear proliferation and the adamant attitude associated with it. Another equally dangerous threat is from environmental degradation and the impending natural catastrophe. Population explosion and the alarming increase in poverty and hunger, deprivation, disparities and socio-economic contradictions at the base of the social structure erodes the health of a majority of the people and the wealth of the developing nations. A group of new generation diseases headed by AIDS is hunting mankind. In addition, the increasing violence, armed conflicts, crimes, corruption and other barbarous and thoughtless activities of man are creating chaotic social conditions in human society. In a nutshell, there is no safety or security on earth.

The new millennium gives us an opportunity to come together, think together and work together to find lasting solutions to various human problems. The world has been searching for lasting peace on earth ever since the first nuclear bomb was dropped at Hiroshima and Nagasaki. But mankind's hope to end fear, hatred, hunger and misery seems to have lost its direction in the fast moving clouds of nuclear proliferation, poverty and pollution. But in spite of the negative results, efforts are on to create a world without fear and without hunger. At the same time, the threats of nuclear weapons, environmental degradation and hunger have created an alarming situation in the world. If we fail in our endeavour to find lasting solutions to human problems, the darkest days of the barbarian age will stage a comeback. Total dedication and commitment of all peoples and countries of the world are indispensable to save mankind from self-destruction.

A shift in the policies of the world and unconditional acceptance of the principles of brotherhood, tolerance, non-violence, non-aggression, peaceful coexistence and respect to human rights and values are *sine qua non* to save mankind from the threat of annihilation. The need of the hour is a change of consciousness among all sections of the population. And the advent of the new millennium is an opportune moment for a change of consciousness. A change of consciousness is the one and only way to save mankind from self-destruction and promote peace and prosperity in the world.

In this book, I have presented a lot of vital information about the crucial problems and challenges confronting mankind. The book helps to understand the reality of human life in the present-day world and the imperative need to promote brotherhood, peace and prosperity everywhere. In a nutshell, the millennium thoughts of the author expressed herein aim at human welfare and progress based on equality, freedom, liberty, justice and fraternity and, finally, peace and prosperity for everyone in the future world.

K. Balan

Contents

1
Self-destruction or Survival— Choice before Mankind

The new millennium has just begun. We should make it an era of peace and prosperity. But the thinking seems to be unfavourable for such a step. The threat of annihilation looms large, as the nuclear proliferation continues. The disastrous consequences of a nuclear war are known to us ever since Hiroshima and Nagasaki were destroyed by nuclear bombs. But today its capacity has increased manifold. If the hatred and ego of man burst into a nuclear war today, it may end in total destruction. At a time when the advance of science and information technology is shaping a global village, use of nuclear and other deadly weapons to destroy mankind and nature would only be a barbarous, suicidal and thoughtless act. In the new millennium, every effort should be directed to help all human beings living on earth to attain the highest possible standard of living. Needless to say, a change of consciousness, a change of attitude, and a change of outlook of man and a major shift in the policies of all nations are *sine qua non* to save mankind and nature from the impending disaster.

Now the choice before mankind is self-destruction or survival. In other words, it is a question of protecting human civilisation or destroying it. Let us ponder this peculiar problem of mankind. What would be the thinking of modern man? What would be the thinking of a cultured man ? What would be the thinking of an illiterate man? If we go on questioning, we will be able to understand the truth. If we think in favour of self-destruction, that will ultimately ruin the human civilisation. If we are opting for survival, then all the nations and peoples of the world should work for peace and prosperity of the entire mankind. This is possible only if we accept the principles of brotherhood, tolerance, friendship and cooperation, non-aggression and peaceful coexistence and total disarmament. The new millennium year is an opportune moment to take the right decision.

Life today is a struggle of man against problems. Problems are increasing day by day. There will be many more new life-threatening problems in the future world. Let us come together, think together and work together to face these problems with courage and conviction. Unless we take up these problems and other connected issues as a challenge and solve them with a commitment, there will be no lasting peace on earth and man's fate will hang in uncertaintly in the new age. So to say, there is need for a political will, democratic spirit, dynamic leadership and collective responsibility to put an end to the present day complex problems. This is essential for the safety, security and progress of man on earth. This can be achieved only if people and countries of the world rise above narrow loyalties, resolve differences, disputes, etc., amicably and work with devotion and oneness of purpose to find lasting solution to the problems facing humanity. This will ensure peace and progress in the new age.

In a nutshell, we should create a world without fear and without hunger, a world where people will freely choose the path of development, a world where there will be ample opportunities to all, a world which will give up high expenditure on war weapons and earmark such funds for the betterment of the people affected by poverty and hunger and finally a world where there will be lasting peace.

So, the earlier we achieve the above goal, the better it will be for mankind. The first step needed in this direction is to strengthen values in human society and recognise the value of human life, wherever and in whatever condition they live.

Educational objectives should be changed by all nations to suit the needs of the future so that the younger generation could be educated to meet the challenges of the changing times. Similarly, the global outlook and the outlook of the people should change towards this objective.

In shaping the future history of man, we must establish a strong and unbreakable social, economic and cultural relationship between nations so that it will pave the way for a new world order. The introduction and modernisation of nuclear and chemical weapons of mass destruction by various countries is the most disturbing factor in modern history. The complex problems of nuclear weapons proliferation can be effectively tackled only with the active cooperation of all nations, particularly the nuclear powers of the world. In order to create a world free of mass destruction nuclear weapons, we should first establish a world order based on the universal principles of equality and justice. The future of man would depend upon how we tackle the problem of nuclear weapons proliferation.

The important step needed in this direction is a consensus for banning nuclear weapons testing and halting production of nuclear materials. Every nation knows the fact that nuclear weapons can destroy mankind and then there should not be any difficulty in reaching a consensus at the global level. International agreements to outlaw the use of nuclear weapons and vigorous negotiations for nuclear disarmament should move fast to create a nuclear-free world.

The most important of all problems in the world today is the threat of nuclear war, cold war, conflicts and confrontations that may lead to war. It took years for man to reach the present growth of nuclear science but it may take only a few minutes to destroy the entire world if it is used for destructive purposes. This is precisely because the growth of nuclear science has taken a major diversion towards destructive weapons and other such purposes, than on peaceful purposes. Big and small wars fought over the years have left scars all over and if we fail to give up monstrous means of mass destruction, that will lead to the annihilation of mankind.

There is, therefore, need for an amicable settlement of all disputes and conflicts between nations. After all, all properties in the world are owned by nature, and, we believe all human beings are created by God, and as such there is no reason why man should fight for properties of nature and kill millions of innocent people instead of helping them to survive and carry out their birth obligation. This can be done successfully if disarmament and non-use of nuclear and chemical weapons is followed by all nations of the world. The method of using force to settle international problems should be discontinued forthwith. We should also remove hatred, mistrust and narrow attitudes from the minds of the people so that there will not be any conflicts that may lead to war. This will instil a sense of confidence in the minds of the people. In this age of information technology, we should be able to solve our problems through discussions and negotiations. Also, we should hold high the banner of peace, freedom and human dignity and all human beings should be benefited by these three rights. Prevention of arms race, halting nuclear tests, and total destruction of nuclear and chemical weapons should be given top priority in the foreign policy of all nations of the world. The future policy should envisage lowering military expenditure and capability, peaceful settlement of all issues, consistent and purposeful efforts to curtail arms race, and international law to check nuclear weapons proliferation. The right of the people for a peaceful and progressive life should be recognised by all.

The need of the new age is to create some kind of a world order which will make the United Nations more powerful and autonomous with powers and supremacy in decision making to create a world free of nuclear and chemical weapons. All member countries of the world should have equal status in the United Nations as a symbol of equality. The global outlook and approach to problems should be on humanitarian grounds. The

United Nations should have the power to halt the killing of innocent people in the name of war or otherwise. The survival of future man on earth would depend upon how we resolve the issues and problems of war, particularly nuclear war. If we fail to do this in a peaceful manner, war is going to be the 'monstrons killer' of the new age. This should be avoided at any cost so that mankind's progress will not be affected. For several decades, the spell of cold war gripped the global community almost completely. There can be no security for anyone in a world bristling with weapons. The world's greatest danger today is nuclear arms race. This must be stopped at any cost. It is a question of survival or death of man on earth. The United Nations will have to play an instrumental role to (1) prevent proliferation of nuclear weapons, (2) ban use of nuclear technology for non-peaceful purpose. and (3) make peaceful coexistence acceptable to all countries of the world with a view to strengthen the foundation of peace in the world for peaceful settlement of all issues, disputes and conflicts between nations and finally bring about a complete Nuclear Test Ban Treaty based on equality. This will lay the foundation for a world, without war and conflicts, and of friendship, goodwill and cooperation among all nations and people. Such a situation will help to make the dream for a world without fear and without hunger a reality in the new age. People and countries irrespective of their place and status of living, should act together to stop the drift towards disaster. Peace, freedom, and economic and social justice concern all people and nations and this goal can be achieved only in a nuclear-free world.

While on the subject, the remarks of the Prime Minister of India contained in his statement at the United Nations 50th Anniversary Special Commemorative Meeting of the General Assembly on October 24, 1995, reading as under, is thought-provoking:

"There can be no security for anyone in a world bristling with nuclear weapons. Deterrence is a false belief. When some possess these weapons for an indefinite time, it becomes a tempting objective for others too, leading consequently to proliferation which is impossible to police for all time. The idea of permanent limited number of nuclear states is thus unrealistic and self-defeating. I would make a fervent appeal to this august body to take credible steps for the complete elimination of all nuclear weapons within a stipulated time-frame. India's action plan presented in 1988 in this behalf could serve as an appropriate starting point. India looks upon it essentially as a proposal inspired by Gandhian principles and is fully committed to it."

Thus, total nuclear disarmament based on a comprehensive and complete ban on nuclear weapons proliferation involving all nations of the world will alone make life on earth safe, peaceful and progressive in the new age. This challenge should be met with a commitment by all nations of the world.

It can be said that without achieving the goal of nuclear disarmament, we cannot establish a world without fear and without hunger. So, this agenda should find a prominent place in the action plan of each and every nation. Then only can we establish a global village with peace and prosperity.

2

Environmental Degradation Endangering Life on Earth

> The first World Environment Day of the new millennium was celebrated on June 5, 2000. The World Environment Day Celebration is an opportune moment for a retrospection. Looking back, we have done a lot to protect the environment. But, unfortunately, the more we protect, the more is the damage done to it. That is the trend of the day. This trend must change. Prior to that, our attitude and behaviour should change. What is needed is an indomitable spirit to make the land, air and water clean. If every person plants one tree a day, 1,000 million people in India can do wonders. That should be our spirit. That will save mankind from the impending environmental catastrophe.

We have been celebrating June 5 every year, as World Environment Day ever since the United Nations Conference on Human Environment was held at Stockholm in June 1972. We do it with much enthusiasm and publicity but not with a commitment to carry on our mission uninterruptedly to protect the environment. Seminars are organised, papers are presented and discussions held on various environmental issues. Newspapers bring out special supplements and the electronic media project an environmental image on that day. But the time has come for self-questioning about our participation in the World Environment Day and its impact on environmental issues. It is an opportunity for all of us to ask ourselves, what do we do to protect the environment? How many people think about it on that day? How many people continue to think about it after the celebration is over? And how many people carry on their environmental mission continuously? And finally, how far do the discussions held and decisions taken on this occasion influence the policy makers? Thus goes the series of crucial questions before mankind today.

According to Dr. Des Griffin, "the purpose of World Environment Day is to give a human face to environmental issues; empower people to become active agents of sustainable and equitable development; promote an understanding that communities are pivotal to changing attitudes towards environmental issues; and advocate partnerships which will ensure all nations and peoples enjoy a safe and prosperous future."

Surprisingly and understandably, if we look at the increasing attack on and damage to nature, it would appear that such celebrations are not taken seriously and the decision taken on that occasion are not influencing the policies on environmental issues to the needed extent. Perhaps, the very purpose of the World Environment Day is considered to be fulfilled with the one-day celebration. People generally feel that all ends with that. That could be the only conclusion one can arrive at, as we see before our very eyes, day in and day out, that the environment is being degraded and the green earth is slowly moving towards a painful death. The environmental degradation has reached an alarming situation and now the only question before mankind is—Preserve the nature or Perish?

"The earth is turning sick, changes in the planet's climate triggered by the greenhouse effect, threaten to jeopardise the human health. Food and fresh water supplies will be disrupted, millions of people displaced and new disease patterns will emerge" writes Mr. George Sanderson in one of the issues of *our planet*—the magazine of the United Nations Environment Programme.

A changing climate and the rising temperature, experts say, would alter the ecosystem of the vectors or agents which carry or cause many diseases, whether these be viruses, bacteria, parasites or snails. It will spread bacterial, viral and parasite diseases and increase alarmingly water borne and air-borne diseases. Experts say diseases like hepatitis B, epidemic cerebral meningitis, polio, cholera and dysentery flourish in a hot and humid weather. The role of environmental degradation in creating immunological deficiency in human beings causing modern diseases like AIDS needs to be probed in the light of the mystery about the disease.

Research in Kenya has brought to light that warming of the climate increases malarial mosquitoes. Thus it could be seen that environmental degradation will have devastating effect on human health.

Nature has started to retaliate and attack life on earth more forcefully than expected. The food shortages in spite of the green revolution in the fields, the emergence of new generation diseases and the increase of health problems alarmingly in spite of tremendous advances in medicine, the decreasing ground water level, the increasing natural calamities and unfriendly changes in climate are indications of an impending catastrophe.

The pollution of air is becoming more curious than ever. The people in the developing countries are the worst affected. The irrepairable damage being done to ozone layer, which protects us from the dangerous ultraviolet rays of the sun, is likely to have a devastating effect on the health of the people and the wealth of the earth. The indiscreet discharge of CFCs by industries continues in the name of development. If we fail to arrest this damage being done to the ozone layer in the upper atmosphere and prevent further damage, the catastrophe ahead will be unbearable to mankind. As a result, there will be alarming increase in global warming, habitat loss, crop failure, species extinction, sea level rise, increased tidal waves and hurricanes, climatic change and new generation diseases.

A lion's share of the pesticides—nearly one-fifth of the global production—reaches the developing countries. Pesticides and chemical poisoning occurs mainly because people handle it without proper precaution and knowledge about the hazards. In an earlier report, WHO said, "our estimates show that the vast majority of acute poisoning occur in an endemic manner in many developing countries with little attention being paid by the local public health researchers." But in the industrialised countries too, harmful residues regularly spill over into foodstuffs and water sources. Unfortunately, chemical transformations, whether through combustion or from other substances, causes environmental pollution. It can be said that the chemicals, fertilisers and pesticides used in the agricultural production is slowly poisoning human beings in developing countries. These countries do not have facilities or means to reduce and control it.

Another major source of urban air pollution is the automobile. The motor vehicles are found guilty for discharging lead, carbon monoxide, nitrogenoxides, etc., which cause extensive damage to the human system. The automobiles also create noise pollution. Needless to say that air pollution caused by automobiles has made man a victim of several diseases.

Emission of various chemicals into the air is a real damage to the ecosystem with serious climatic consequences and changes that may make human life impossible on earth in the distant future. In India and other developing countries, a lot of discharge from chemical factories and automobile take shelter in the atmosphere. We will be able to understand the damage correctly if we look at the remark in the *Human Development Report 1998* reading as "Brazil, China, India and Mexico are among the developing countries with the highest emissions. ...

The human consequences of the global warming from carbon dioxide will be devastating for many poor countries—with a rise in sea levels, Bangladesh could see its land area shrink by 17%."

The invisible radiation is another threat to mankind. It is not possible to exactly assess the amount of radiation leaking into the water, soil and air from the present sources and from accidents. The tragedies and after-effects of accidents in England, USSR, USA, France and West Germany are well known. There is an urgent need to prevent accidents of nuclear plants and leaking of radiation. Needless to say, gas and chemicals leaked out after accidents are also causing damages to the environment. In India the wounds of Bhopal tragedy is yet to heal. It is still green in the memory of the affected people.

There has been largescale destruction of forests all over the world. Replanting of trees was not as fast as the deforestation. As a result, the world's forests are shrinking speedily endangering all living beings on earth. The magnitude of the problem can be judged from the observation in the *Human Development Report 1998* reading as "Deforestation is concentrated in developing countries. Over the last two decades, Latin America and the Caribbean lost seven million hectares of tropical forest, Asia and Sub-Saharan Africa 4 million hectares each."

Thus the fast moving deforestation to meet the human development needs and the inadequacy of replanting to undo the damage is causing environmental damage and devastation all over the world. If the situation continues, the aftermath of it will be unbearable to mankind and other living beings on earth.

The effluents and wastes from industry released into the sea and the fumes, smoke and gas poured out from distilleries, refineries, chemical plants, etc., polluting the atmosphere, bring life-threatening calamities to mankind.

The frequent climatic change resulting from environmental degradation and the consequent natural calamities cost the nation about eight thousand crores of rupees a year, apart from loss of life. Floods caused by sea level rise and other natural calamities, inundate low lying areas, sewerage and sanitary systems spreading infectious diseases. It also causes extensive damage to crops.

Noise pollution is increasing day by day. Noise is an invisible health hazard causing various ailments in the human body, which include hearing defects, neurosis, mental illness, peptic ulcer, irritation, fatigue, allergy, cardiovascular diseases, etc. Research studies have brought to light that continuous exposure to intolerable noise can cause these diseases. An environmental expert has remarked that if the noise level continues at the present rate, most people living in major metropolises will be deaf by the year 2050. The findings of the research study by Dr. Surya Kant Mishra in Kanpur indicate that school children are the worst sufferers of noise pollution. According to his findings, 60 per cent of students in noise polluted areas fail to concentrate in the class, 40 per cent suffer from hearing problems and a significant number of them complain of headache and irritation.

The main sources of noise are loudspeakers, road and rail traffic, aircraft and industrial units, fire crackers and homes. Research studies in India have indicated an intolerable level of noise in Delhi and Mumbai measuring between 60 decibels and 105 decibels. Noise pollution at home emanating from conversation, quarrel, utensils, food mixer, television, radio etc., sometimes rise to intolerable levels.

Noise pollution is easy to control. It should be regulated at source by proper education and behaviour. Rigid rules and stringent punishment for violation of rules are also necessary.

The reasons for other types of environmental degradation are many and varied. Both individuals and organisations contribute their share towards this problem. Some of the causes are unplanned population growth, largescale migration to urban areas with about 30 per cent of urban population living in slums, felling of trees in forests, overcrowded residential areas, destruction of water sources, lack of sewerage and drainage, dumping of wastes and use of dangerous fertilisers and pesticides.

Paradoxically, irrepairable damage is being done by effluent gases like sulphur dioxide, nitrogen dioxide, hydrogen sulphide, carbon monoxide, lead from automobile exhausts, arsenic cadmium and selenium, etc., and other particles discharged from industries and other sources. Air and soil wastes wash down and pollute lakes, pounds, rivers, tanks, wells and other sources of water. Sewage and untreated industrial wastes are finding their way to holy rivers in a big way.

India receives more than one and a half times the rainfall that other parts of the world get and 80 per cent of it is in four months of the monsoon season. India also has the largest number of rivers in the world. But, unfortunately, majority of the rural people do not get clean and safe drinking water. In some parts there is plenty and in many other parts there is acute water scarcity. This is due to lack of scientific methods for proper storage and equitable distribution of water. Pollution of drinking water, over-utilisation and waste of water where it is available in plenty are also important reasons for decreasing ground water level and shortage of drinking water. It has been reported that 80 per cent of the diseases in rural areas are caused by polluted water and unhygienic surroundings. Research findings in the US indicate that chlorinated water is a high risk factor of cancer.

The water in almost all rivers in India stands polluted at varying degrees. This is caused by both human wastes and industrial wastes. The following report in the *Human Development Report 1998* (page 69) (Sampat 1996) is an eye opener to us. It, *inter alia*, reads:

> "Supporting a staggering 400 million people along its 1,560 mile course, the Ganges forms the most populous river basin in the world with about 1,000 people per mile. Today, there are more than 29 cities, 70 towns and thousands of villages along the Ganges banks, depositing nearly all their sewage—more than 1.3 billion litres a day— directly into the river. Another 260 million litres of industrial waste are added to this by the hundreds of factories along the river's banks. All the waste enters the river largely untreated. To the raw sewage and factory effluents are added the runoff from more than 6 million tons of chemical fertiliser and some 9,000 tons of pesticides."

Forests in developing countries, particularly in India, are shrinking rapidly. It is estimated that at least one-fifth of the forests has been lost over the years. As the deforestation by greedy man goes on, the forest wealth is decreasing with no effort to undo the damage. So much so, greenery areas are fast turning into dry lands in India. Even the tourists are surprised when they see high concrete buildings in place of green and beautiful landscape. Soil erosion caused by felling of trees is a great loss to the nation.

During the second half of the 20th century, India has made tremendous development and economic progress. But there is no disputing the fact that our development has been mostly at the cost of the poor and the environment. As a matter of fact, development increased poverty and deepened the environmental degradation. Needles to say, development without recognising the importance and right of the environment, has brought heavy loss to the nation. The development cost incurred over the years has not taken into account the cost of soil, air, water and forests, which were used, polluted, damaged or degraded in the process of development. This cost may run to several million US dollars every year. The cost incurred to treat diseases caused by environmental degradation has also not been accounted for. For instance, the following observation in the *Human Development Report 1998*

(Page 79) would reveal the magnitude of the cost lost due to environmental pollution. It reads:

> "Economic development has been the watchword in India's march into the 21st century. But the country may bepaying an enormous price for this march, which has brought in its wake ecological devastation and numerous health problems. A conservative estimate of environmental damage puts the figure at more than $10 billion a year, or 4.5 per cent of GDP in 1992. If higher estimates are used, the total environmental costs would be $13.8 billion, or 6 per cent of the GDP. A breakdown of the conservative cost estimate of $10 billion shows that urban air pollution costs India $1.3 billion a year. Water degradation leads to health costs amounting to $5.7 billion every year, nearly three-fifths of the total environmental costs. Soil erosion affects 83.163 million hectares of land every year. Land degradation causes productivity loss equal to 4-6.3% of the total agricultural output every year—the loss amounting to $2.4 billion. And deforestation which proceeded at the rate of 0.6 per cent a year between 1981 and 1990, leads to annual costs of $214 million. These estimates, however, do not include the major environmental costs that arise out of biodiversity loss or pollution due to hazardous wastes". (Agarwal 1996)."

Now, the ecosystem is heading for a breakdown, People of all nationalities, region, culture, races, and economic status will be affected by such a catastrophe. There is no way out to escape except take quick action to prevent further damage to the ecosystem. The ball is now in the people's court. People should be responsible in tackling the environmental problems. Their attitude and behaviour should change for the better. That is the first and most important step needed in this regard. The sooner it happens, the better it will be. We must work hard with total dedication to face the formidable challenges thrown out by environmental degradation. Environment education is the best means to achieve this goal. It should move from mind to mind changing the attitude and behaviour of man in favour of nature.

The government will have to make the people aware of the serious consequences of environmental degradation. There is need for rigid laws to regulate, control and prevent environmental degradation. There is no doubt that the non-government organisations are required to play an instrumental role in providing right leadership to the people. Environmental education should also be introduced in all educational institutions. There should also be programmes to educate the illiterate people. The media has to play an important role in educating people. The primary objective of environment education should be to bring about favourable changes in attitude and behaviour towards environment.

Needless to say that the panchayati raj institutions are required to play a key role to prevent environmental degradation. It should ensure that all future developments are environment-friendly and human-friendly. Panchayati raj institutions should carry out only sustainable and equitable development. Being the custodian of most of the greenary areas of the land, the panchayati raj institutions should ensure that all laws related to environment are enforced in a result-oriented manner. Preserving environment for a better tomorrow should be our goal.

Panchayati raj institutions should organise frequent awareness programmes, pollution check-up camps of vehicles, tree planting programmes, cleanliness drive, supply of safe drinking water, green-productivity awareness programmes; and environmental education programmes. The short-term and long-term programmes of the local bodies will help to minimise the environmental degradation. Such programmes should be organised in partnership with the government departments, voluntary organisations and the community to get satisfactory results.

The increased economic output to meet the growing demands, particularly of the additional population, should be met through environment-friendly development. In this regard, we should be guided by the words of Gandhiji: "Earth provides enough to satisfy every man's need but not for every man's greed." What is happening at the global level to protect environment should simultaneously come to all villages and towns. People should come together and work together in partnership with the government, panchayats, and voluntary organisations to prevent environmental degradation. Now, the choice before mankind is "A dry earth to perish or a green earth to prosper."

The immediate victims of the environmental degradation will be the majority of the poor people in the developing and least developed countries. The personal sufferings, increased poverty, health problems, inequalities and injustice, social disintegration, economic backwardness, derogation of human dignity and misery of the poor people living at the bottom of the society will increase manifold posing a threat to human survival. Will the 20th century advances in science and technology help the world to prevent this calamity? This is an unanswered question before the civilised mankind.

As can be observed from the studies and reports, the danger caused by environmental pollution is fast moving to cross the line of control. It is, therefore, imperative that remedial action and preventive measures must be intensified without any loss of time. The basis of a result-oriented action plan will be the political will and commitment of each country. Active support of the Global Agencies are equally important. In addition, there should be well-planned and effective education and awareness campaign to make each and every individual realise the serious consequences and life-and-death threat from environmental pollution. Each and every individual should contribute his share to strengthen the movement against environmental pollution and damage to the natural systems endangering human life. "DEVELOPMENT WITHOUT POLLUTION" should be the slogan in the new century.

As a result of education and awareness created by various agencies and newspapers, the link between the quality of environment and quality of public health is being widely realised by the public. In developed nations, attempts are being made to reduce the harmful pollutions emitted by cars by running them on lead-free petrol, and fitting them with catalysers to reduce the output of carbon monoxide.

In countries with a lesser standard of living, the facilities to control air pollution are far from adequate. People in these countries are victims of air pollution. Drastic measures are necessary to control and reduce the effect of pollution on human life.

WHO, together with UN Environmental Programme, keeps a permanent check on air pollution levels through a number of monitoring sites scattered all over the world. Energy production and consumption are routinely blamed for air pollution. We should produce the sources of solar energy and wind power in place of fossil fuels, so that it will help a lot in controlling environmental pollution. The nuclear power industry is a potential source of power but it has a bad image due to accidents and levels of radioactive materials.

Available data show that about 625 million people live in urban areas where the average levels of sulphur dioxide in the air is very high. In fact, sulphur dioxide in the emissions worldwide are increasing by four per cent per year. For the people in the city, this affects seriously the respiratory tract and high concentrations of sulphur dioxide can be lethal. Meanwhile, acid rain results in the death of trees, the pollution of lakes which kills the creatures that live in them; and infiltration of chemicals into the soil and ground water resources. Acid rains can be carried by winds hundreds of miles from the place of origin. Thus, acid rain is becoming a source of pollution. The airborne particles from the desert dust are another threat to environment.

The global air pollution trends clearly show the high risk of pollution in developing countries. In developed countries, there has been a declining trend in sulphur dioxide levels. The world's increasing population felled more and more trees and destroyed forests for household needs. As a result, there are insufficient trees to digest the excess carbon dioxide in the air.

The global greenhouse effect started to take shape. Chloroflurocarbons (CFC's), which are multi-purpose chemicals, have made themselves useful as coolants in refrigerators and as propellant gases for aerosol cans. They are widely used in electronics and in plastic-foam materials. When the CFCs are set free, they become a menace to the environment. They damage and eat away the upper ozone layer and contribute to the greenhouse effect. Consequent upon this, the earth is exposed to the dangers of ultraviolet radiation. These rays damage the living cells, cause sunburn, increase the incidence of skin cancer throughout the world and lower agricultural production through changing climate. Global warming and the depletion of the ozone layer could prove to be calamitous of the worst kind in the new age. As a result of warming up, if the overall temperature rises, the polar ice caps will start to melt and consequently the sea level will rise exposing several countries to various problems. The global agricultural production will be disturbed threatening the food supply. Ultimately, the development achieved by decades of efforts will crumble down.

This is a calamity of humankind's own making. Having known about its serious consequences, the people and countries of the world should work hard to save the world from this calamity

In a nutshell, it can be said that the entire world is today under the clouds of dangerous environmental pollution. Man should have kept out nature and environment, without any damage due to developmental activities, for the benefit of the present and future generations. The achievement in science and technology should have included some kind of 'checks and controls' to save the world from environmental pollution during the course of its development. But this was not done to the extent needed. The result is uncontrollable growth of pollution, which today threatens to wipe out mankind from the earth. The pollution generated by industry, which is a major source of pollution in the world, can be fully controlled by accepting the concept of 'Green productivity' by all countries of the world and implementing it in every industry.

Thus the serious problems of (1) over-population, poverty and hunger, (2) nuclear weapons proliferation and (3) the environmental pollution should be solved on a war-footing to save the future generations from degeneration and destruction. Unless and until we solve these problems, we will not be able to establish a "world without fear and without hunger" in the new age or make it an age of peace and prosperity.

3

Child Welfare—New Century Perspectives

Today's children, they say, are the seeds of the next generation. So the quality of the people of the new generation would depend upon the quality of the children of today. But we do not appear to have recognised it. This is evident from the present situation. During the 20th century there has been an undeclared war on children. It appears that the most heinous crime of the century was committed against children. Millions of children were killed, injured and displaced in armed conflicts. According to Global Agencies, about 540 million children, i.e., one in every four in the world, is living below the poverty line. The working children in Asian countries come to about 250 million. In a nutshell, the majority of the children in developing world are victims of poverty, hunger, malnutrition, exploitation, discrimination, illiteracy, cruelty, child labour, violence, armed conflicts, unsafe environment, inequality and social instability. Let us remember that the abysmally low quality of children is bound to reflect very hadly on the quality of the new generation. The time has come for us to open our eyes, understand the reality and work with total dedication to mould today's children as capable inheritors of mankind.

The spirit, enthusiasm and momentum of the new millennium should be used to serve the suffering children in the world. We must formulate long-term plans to save the majority children in the developing world from dangerous living conditions and mould them as capable citizens of the future. Every individual, every family, every nation and the world as a whole is responsible and accountable for child welfare and development, as it concerns with the future of mankind on earth.

The first World Children's Day of the new millennium was celebrated on 24 February 2000. It was indeed an occasion to study the present state of the children and formulate long-term master plans for proper development of the majority children who are living in a miserable condition. In other words, it is high time for an honest introspection with a view to understand the magnitude of the problem and plan a better future for the suffering children. Such an exercise in right earnest would reveal that the most heinous crime of the civilised and educated man was committed against children. It is deplorable and most heinous a crime because the children, being mentally and physically weak, are unable to resist or adequately respond to the atrocities perpetrated on them . As a result, they are destined to live in a miserable and dehumanising condition. There is no disputing the fact that the cruelty and crime on children undermines our progress and civilisation. What is happening in the world of children is a gross violation of the human rights and rights of the children adopted in the United Nations Convention on the rights of the children held in 1989 and the World Summit on Children held in 1990.

Although the 20th century brought epoch-making progress to human civilisation, the last ten years of the century witnessed an undeclared war on children, adolescents and women. For them, it was a war between life and death, as poverty, violence, conflicts, exploitation, social instability, unsafe environment and diseases threatened their rights and sabotaged their progress. According to UNICEF the majority children in developing countries endure a life of hunger, malnutrition, exploitation, violence and illness. Surprisingly and understandably, they are denied basic human rights such as nutritious food, shelter, safe environment, adequate health care, freedom, equality and justice, which they are entitled to like any other children. Now the crucial question before civilised mankind is whether the advance of science and technology is capable of helping these children to live and grow in the right direction like the children in the upper strata of the society.

Every great man on earth had said that today's children are the makers and guardian of the future. And that is the truth. But there is no safe place for poor children in this world today. So we have to create a safe environment for them in this world. Every individual, every community, every nation and the world as a whole should ensure that the children, wherever they live, are well protected, properly cared, looked after, educated, trained and moulded as disciplined, potential and intelligent citizens of the future. Obviously, the parents and teachers have to play an instrumental role in providing them proper guidance and safe environment at home and school respectively.

Paradoxically, the majority of the children in the lower strata of the society, are not getting opportunities for growth. They are often misguided or confused over their future. We have failed to provide them a safe environment. Of the total child population, only one-third is getting opportunities for decent living. In spite of the assurance of rights and privileges, protection, equality and justice by every nation and Global Agencies, thousands of children are thrown out of the civilised society and destined to live in miserable and unsafe condition, sometimes, at sub-human level. The seriousness of the situation can be viewed with the fact that as many as 540 million children, i.e., one in every four children in the world, live in dangerous and unstable situations. Of the 1.2 billion people in the world living below the poverty line with earning less than one dollar per day, 600 million are children.

What is really shocking and barbaric is the exploitation of children during the armed conflicts. According to statistics in the *state of the World's Children 2000*, during the last ten years of the 20th century alone, about two million children were killed, six million seriously injured or disabled, one million orphaned and 15 million children displaced and made refugees in the various armed conflicts. In addition, about 8,000 to 10,000 children are killed or maimed by landmines every year.

In South-east Asia alone, every year millions of girls are born into poverty, debt servitude and dehumanising conditions. In India, female foeticide due to social prejudice is high. It has been reported that as many as one million girls in the world are caught in the nets of commercial sex exploiters every year. In the poor families and communities, women including girls fall victims to isolation, illiteracy, exploitation and inhuman treatment. According to reports, in South Asia alone, girls and boys numbering between 20 and 40 million toil in debt servitude of their parents. According to ILO, there are about 250 million working children in the age group of 5 to 14 years in developing countries at the end of the century and 50 to 60 million children in the age group of 5 to 14 work in hazardous circumstances.

Also, there was alarming increase in child destitutes/ orphans, and street children. As a matter of fact, grown up people particularly the educated, have been forcing children into domestic servitude, sexual exploitation, pornography and trafficking of drugs. Besides tens of thousands of children are victims of natural calamities, home violence and manmade calamities. Thus, it could be seen that driving children into the worst forms of labour, hazardous work, obscure and dangerous world was the most heinous crime in the civilised society.

In the health front, the situation is more curious than ever. The majority of the children in developing and least developed countries are falling victims to a series of modern diseases headed by HIV/AIDS, Hepatitis B, etc. Non-availability of safe drinking water and essential food, and healthy shelter, unhygenic living conditions are the main reasons for the health problems of poor children. In case of poor children in developing countries, malnutrition and killer diseases are causing serious concern. In poor countries, lack of facilities for timely immunisation and treatment leads to increased death of children. While immunisation is available to prevent major killer diseases, the recent reports of the failure of oral polio, BCG, Hepitat B vaccines are causing concern in some quarters.

And today, in spite of all medical advances, a majority of the children in poor countries are threatened by modern diseases like HIV/AIDS. It has been reported that each day 8,500 children and young people around the world are infected by HIV and 2,500 women die from AIDS. According to global reports, in 1998 alone the number of women killed by HIV/AIDS was 9,00,000. In India, the mortality rate still remains at 410 per lakh births and about 30 per cent of the new births are underweight due to malnutrition. In developing countries, a large number of children are killed by tetanus infection.

Of the six billion population in the world, around one billion is children and another one billion adolescents aged between 10 and 19. But the majority of them are living in developing world in an environment threatened by poverty, malnutrition, killer diseases, exploitation, violence, illiteracy and discrimination. They do not get opportunities to develop their skill and potential and use their energy for the betterment of mankind. So, if the majority children and members of the younger generation in poor countries are not given opportunities for proper education and development, mankind will lose a lot. Perhaps that may even lead to the break down of the human civilisation. It is often said that today's children are tomorrow's nation builders, but living in a poor and dangerous environment and with no opportunities for education and employment, how these teeming millions can grow and become partners of progress is debatable. Relevant here is the well known proverb: "in a healthy body, there lives a healthy mind", and if we are unable to keep the majority poor children in the world in good health, how can we give them a healthy mind, a growing mind and a progressive mind to shoulder the future tasks and responsibilities of building a new generation.

Summing up, it could be seen that the last quarter of the 20th century witnessed alarming increase in (1) forced child labour (2) commercial sexual exploitation of children (3) female foeticide (4) domestic violence, rapes and forced pregnancies of girls (5) armed conflicts and violence involving children (6) rude home behaviour towards children (7) production and trafficking of drugs using children (8) children's illness and neglect, and (9) accidents and assaults involving children. Insensitiveness to and a callous attitude towards the problems of children is a matter of serious consequences. Looking at the real state of them in the developing world, we are forced to believe that the greatest crime of the civilised man during the 20th century was directed against children.

The basic reasons for the above problems involving children could be identified as (1) absence of a national agenda for protection, education and development of children as a national asset (2) poverty and unhygenic living conditions of family (3) increased anti-social and inhuman activities in society (4) leadership failure at family and community level (5) lack of vision (6) absence of moral and social values and social consciousness (7) absence of love and disregard of the rights of the children (8) lack of opportunities for education, employment and growth (9) improper guidance, and (10) social and economic insecurity.

In India, the problems associated with children are increasing at alarming rates year after year. For instance, every day in India 48,000 children are born and one-third of them weigh only half of what the normal children weigh. To accommodate the newcomers, we need about 90,000 additional primary schools every year. And all facilities of life should be made available to them when they grow up. There is, therefore, a need for a clear vision on the future of children.

Therefore, what is needed is meticulous planning from the childhood stage onwards. Then, we will be able to mould the children as useful and potential citizens of tomorrow. This will save them from neglect and cruelty. In this regard, the words of Theo-Ben Gurirab are worth remembering. In the opening remarks to the 54th General Assembly of the United Nations, Theo-Ben Gurirab, Foreign Minister of Namibia and President of the Assembly, identified the future of children as one of the main challenges fạcing the world "...their lives are at daily risk of being snatched away by the cruelty and indifference of adults."

As the 21st century begins, a clearer and surer sense should prevail on every grown up individual and every home, every community, every region and every nation and the world as a whole to formulate a definite agenda that works. Such an agenda in the 'UN Year 2000 of Culture and Peace' should, *inter alia*, aim at protecting the rights of the children and promoting their health, education, development and well being; so that they can be effective players and active workers of the future society.

In this connection, the following indicators are important:

a) Mother's health is very important to ensure good care to children. So, the health and well-being of the mother should receive priority.

b) Every child should be ensured better transition to primary/adolescent stage.

c) Early childhood care, good character and behaviour are critical factors to the child's subsequent transition to adulthood.

d) Research has proved that physical, mental and cognitive development in an individual would depend on the good nutrition, love and guidance in the early years of life.

e) The growth and development of the child should cover

physical, emotional, spiritual and intellectual aspects of his personality.

f) Stringent punishment should be meted out to those who commit crime and cruelty against children.

g) Legislative measures must be taken to enforce the rights of the children.

h) Attention should be paid to bring down drastically the mortality rate for children, and maternal deaths.

i) Protection from malnutrition among children under five, immunisation of all children against killer diseases, education to all children, easy access to safe water and sanitation, protected shelter and safe environment, improved health and medical facilities and prevention of all crime and cruelty involving children are other factors that need to be taken care of.

As the new millennium begins, the majority of the people who live in poverty are women and children. They are the most vulnerable to conflicts, violence, infection, exploitation and abuse. Their rights and privileges are being ignored by educated and civilised persons. There is no exaggerating the fact that children today are threatened by poverty, inequality, injustice, conflicts, violence and discrimination. Ultimately, today's children can grow up as the future nation builders only if we ensure that they are capable, intelligent and self-reliant. Every family, every community and every nation should be aware of and concerned with all problems of child development. It is an inescapable responsibility. The adolescent population should have the knowledge, skills, attitudes, outlook and commitment to work individually and collectively to solve the problems of mankind.

The message of Kofi A. Annan, Secretary General of the United Nations, published in *The State of World's Children 2000* is an eye-opener to all nations and peoples. It, *inter alia*, reads:

> There is no trust more sacred than the one the world holds with children. There is no duty more important than ensuring that their rights are respected and their welfare is protected and their lives are free from fear and want and that they grow up in peace. The state of the world's children is a rallying call to us all. It is a call to governments, civil society, the private sector and the whole international community to renew our commitments to children's rights by advancing a new vision for the 21st century; a vision in which every infant has a healthy beginning, every child a quality education and adolescent the opportunity to develop his or her unique abilities. It is a call to families and communities and the children and adolescents themselves to make their voices heard in helping translate this vision to reality in their daily lives.

If we imbibe the spirit of this message, it will help us to stop cruelty and crime against children, and enrich their lives with values to mould them as strong pillars of future society. To achieve success in this direction, we need a dedicated mind, a commitment and readiness to shoulder the social responsibility entrusted to every man by nature. It is high time that we begin our work with a pledge to meet our commitment honestly.

It is an acknowledged fact that in the developing countries, children are physically, mentally, intellectually and psychologically at a sub-standard level. In spite of the good work done by the governments and organisations right from the United Nations down to the village level voluntary organisations, we are unable to solve the multi-faceted problems of children, and meet the challenges of their development. A large number of children are not benefited by the legislations, global conventions and national planning. Apparently, the children in the developing world and poor countries are not able to get the benefits brought about by development.

When rockets pierce the sky, a number of children in the developing world are begging for a piece of bread. That is the plight of the children who are fighting for survival at the base of the society. With the birth of 3,54,000 new babies (approx) every day, the challenges and problems of child development are becoming formidable. It is therefore essential that each and every individual, family, community, government, educational institution and Non-Governmental Agencies should share the responsibility and challenges of child development in an equitable manner. Then only, will there be capable inheritors for future. All of us should redouble our efforts in this direction. It is our indomitable spirit, our dedication, our love to the poor children, our social consciousness, our ability to understand others' feeling, our desire for social service that matters more than anything else to achieve success in our endeavour. That can no doubt light the ray of hope and progress in the life of poor children living with us in a miserable condition.

The developing countries are too late in formulating a clear, human-friendly child policy. At least at the beginning of the new millennium every nation should have a national policy on children to plan, control and monitor their growth, education, character, well-being and development and create sufficient opportunities for adolescents to use their knowledge and energy for nation building. Such a national policy should incorporate all global plans, resolutions and legislations formulated or suggested to protect the rights of the children and promote their well-being. The National Child Policy may include the following factors:

1. Small family concept and package for better health of the children. Guidelines for better health and character formation at home and school.
2. Declaring each child as a national asset. Equality and justice should be the basic factors.
3. Special package for homeless, poor and destitute children.
4. Rigid rules to stop all atrocities, crimes, discrimination and exploitation involving children, and stringent punishment for such crimes.

5. Special package to protect children from poverty, malnutrition, illiteracy and diseases.
6. Legislative measures to regulate and control exposure of children to such programmes and advertisements in the electronic media which cripple the behaviour and character formation of children.
7. Rigid control to save children from drugs, alcohol and tobacco use, which are harmful to their health and future life.
8. Clear out policy guidelines governing each and every adolescent to enable them to get professional education and employment and opportunities to work.
9. Increasing the responsibility and accountability of educational institutions, panchayati raj institutions and, non-governmental organisations in all matters concerning the education, development and well-being of children.

The year 2000 is the United Nations Year of Culture and Peace. It is an opportune time for us to make a new beginning, a new approach and a new vision for the protection, education, well-being and development of children in the right direction that will make their future bright and the future of mankind safe and prosperous.

Healthy Children—A Happier World

Healthy children are essential for a happy family. A happy world cannot result from unhealthy children. But we have to move fast and make our children healthy to achieve the goal.

Today a child born in South Asian countries is 20 times more likely to die than a child born in developed countries. Out of every 100 children born in Asian countries, ten die before their first birthday. The heavy load of child illness in developing countries affects the child's growth. So, we are unable to develop their full physical and mental potential.

Diarrhoea is the leading cause of child death in developing countries. About five million children die annually each year due to various diseases like TB, diphtheria, whooping cough, poliomyelitis, tetanus and measles.

The following areas are important to make the child healthy and happy:

1. Timely use of oral rehydration therapy to treat cases of diarrhoea.
2. Continued feeding with breast milk, cooked cereals and banana.
3. Preventing malnutrition in children.
4. Timely immunisation.
5. Safe water.
6. Personal hygiene and cleanliness.
7. Preventing home accidents.

The family and home environment influence the development of moral and physical powers in children. Better results in child care can be achieved only with proper parental planning. Their attitude and behaviour towards the health of the children are most important to achieve success in this direction.

To achieve the goal of healthy children, the family, the teachers, the health workers and the community will have to play an important role. The following areas are important.

1. Create awareness about the health of the children among the people.
2. Advocate the cause from the grassroots level to policy makers.
3. Spread knowledge and information on child health through all available channels.
4. Train a large number of health workers for the rural areas.

5. Provide quality health services.
6. Introduce health education in all educational institutions.

The health and behaviour of the mother are most important aspects for the child's health. So, the health of the mother and the child should be protected.

Many children in developing countries suffer from physical and mental deprivation. This creates in them behavioural disorders and unsocial habits. This can be prevented only with the active involvement of the family and the community.

Mankind owes the child the best it has to give.

Declaration of the Rights of the Child adopted by United Nations on 2 November 1959 states that the child has the right to:

1. Enjoy special protection and get opportunity to develop a healthy and normal manners and conditions of freedom and dignity.
2. Have a name and nationality.
3. Enjoy the benefits of social security including nutrition, housing, recreation and medical services.
4. Receive special treatment, education and care if handicapped.
5. Grow up in an atmosphere of affection and security.
6. Receive education.
7. Receive protection and relief in times of devastation.
8. Be protected against all forms of cruelty, neglect and exploitation.
9. Be protected against discrimination.

The child shall be brought up in an atmosphere of understanding, tolerance, friendship, peace and brotherhood.

This should be our guiding spirit. We should always remember that a healthy child is a healthy family and a healthy nation. (*Source*: *The State of the World's Children 2000*, UNICEF)

4

Education for Tomorrow

Mankind is facing the threat of self-destruction. The rapid increase in man-made calamities and utter disregard for human feelings and values in our society indicate an impending catastrophe. As the quality of mind deteriorates, there is degeneration in every human activity. The fault lies not with the human beings but with those who provided them guidance. Obviously, the most important reason is the failure of education to inculcate in them human values and qualities. This has created more weakness than strength in their personality. And the most disastrous of all is the negative and rebellious attitude being developed in children. Keeping in view the dangers ahead, it is high time we change the concept and purpose of education, to enable it to play its right role in shaping the destiny of man. The harmonious atmosphere and the sanctity of the 'temples of learning' should be restored forthwith. The misunderstanding in the field of education must go and it should be treated as a patriotic and constitutional duty. The one and the only goal of education should be man-making. Educational emancipation is a prerequisite to socio-economic emancipation. The teachers should provide the right leadership to achieve the goal. Every student is a genius and the teacher should strive hard to develop his potential, awaken hidden talents, and empower people. This will help to generate energy, foster development and protect the rights of the people.

In spite of the marvellous progress in the field of education, we have not been able to shape an educational system for the future. Over the years, we have slowly lost its real purpose and direction. Reports produced by various commissions for reform of education were many and varied. But how much of it we have taken in our system is a matter for self-questioning. Education has also failed to reach at least 50 per cent of the population in developing countries.

Education, experts say, is a powerful and fundamental force in the life of man. It plays an instrumental role in shaping the destiny of the individual and the future of mankind. Education, as a value-generating force in society, rejuvenates the present civilisation and lays the foundation for a future one.

Education is expected to play a crucial role in moulding the character of the individual, developing his unique potential and safeguarding the social, moral and spiritual values in society, which indeed are the pillars of any civilisation. To put it in the words of Mahatma Gandhi, the Father of the Nation, "A proper and harmonious combination of body, mind and spirit is required for the making of the whole man and constitutes the true economics of education."

Needless to say, education should contribute not only to the intellectual growth but also equally to the moral, spiritual and physical development of man and then only can it achieve its true goal of man-making.

In this light, the process of education or the action of education is important. And to understand what true educational process is, we should consider the words of Dr. Malcolm S. Adiseshiah which reads:

> Education is the learning process plus the infrastructure for learning—schools, colleges, libraries, museums and all institutions where a learning experience can be had. The learning process is a complex, individual, internalised, interrelated series comprising thinking, reasoning, analysing, inventing, conceptualising, and

> synthesising in which the student and the teacher act and react to each other and the infrastructure. The infrastructure in turn is increasing and expanding and includes today the sports field, the project work; the radio, the film and the many other cultural agencies, and institutions springing up in every educational centre.

So much so, all these activities are imperative and important to achieve the true goal of education, i.e., man-making. But the crucial question is, Are we moving on the right track to carry out the man-making work of education?

The common goal of education aimed at in the 21st century is "Education for all." This goal was set by the nine high population countries in what is known as "Delhi Declaration" signed at the New Delhi Conference on December 16, 1993.

"Only the educated are free," said the great philosopher Epictetus a long time ago. In the philosopher's view, India is not yet free with as many as 450 million or 30 per cent of the world's total illiterates groping in the dark. But we can bail out of the philosopher's view, when we see that the Constitution of the Indian Republic, as a matter of right, enjoins upon the government to provide free and compulsory education to all children. But we are yet to achieve this goal. We have to go miles and miles to reach the goal. At this juncture, when education for all is the talk of the new century, our Constitutional goal is very important. In this light, we are reminded of the words of Jawaharlal Nehru, the architect of modern India: "Given opportunities, India can produce hundreds of thousands of absolutely first-class people in various branches of work and knowledge. But the people do not have these opportunities. Nothing saddens me so much as the sight of children who are denied education, sometimes, denied even food and clothing. If our children are denied education, what is our India of tomorrow going to be ? It is the duty of the state to provide good education for every child in the country. And I would add that it is the duty of the state to provide free education to every child in the country."

But, our vision for the 21st century should not only be 'education for all' by providing good education, but also to create a learning society, and a global society, which will be the need of the new century. This can be achieved only by broadening the perspectives of education, improving the quality of education and making life long learning a way of life.

In our society, education has become a general exercise of mind, and partially a skill-making exercise. Moreover, only about 55 per cent of the population get opportunities for education. And after 15 years of knowledge giving and skill-making process, many have to wait for years to get the opportunity to work. So much so, as could be seen from the statistics, a large number of educated youth are either under-utilised or unutilised. As a result, their energy drains away and that way our nation loses precious energy, which should have otherwise gone for nation building. As the depending population increases year after year, the working population decreases, this trend should be changed for the better. And to achieve this end, the very objective of education should change making it more effective and result-oriented. The energy of the educated should be fruitfully and fully utilised for national development.

The first and foremost influencing factor in the quality of education is 'the teacher'. It is not the material that goes into the mind of children alone that matters but it is the method, the technique, quality and the spirit of teaching that matters most in moulding the character and shaping the future of the tender population of India and the nation. It was because of this fact that teachers enjoyed high respect and command in society from time immemorial. Those were the days when teaching was considered as a noble profession, nay, even today in some countries the place of a teacher is very high. This reveals how the future of the people in that country and the destiny of the nation are being planned.

In our own society, for one reason or another, the glory and greatness of the teaching occupation is fast disappearing. With the education acquiring commercial hue and due to a variety of socio-political and man-made reasons, the command and respect enjoyed by teachers, and the glory of the teaching profession has declined to alarming proportions, particularly in the post-independent period. They are today the most worried people with a lot of problems encircling them which makes their duty difficult and insignificant. It is vital that this should change rapidly for the better. Then only will we be able to restore the glory and greatness of the teaching profession, without which we cannot achieve the real goal of education.

Relevant here is the inspiring and awakening message of Guru Rabindranath Tagore:

> A teacher can never truly teach unless he is still learning himself. A lamp can never light another unless it continues to burn its own flame. The teacher who has come to the end of his subject, who has no living traffic with his knowledge but merely repeats his lessons to his students can only load their minds; he cannot quicken them. Truth not only must inform but also must inspire. If the inspiration dies out and information only accumulates, then truth loses its infinity. The greater part of our learning in the schools has been wasted because, for most of our teachers their subjects are like dead specimens of once-living things, with which they have learned acquaintance but no communication of life or love.

Teachers, they say, are the real makers of the future man. They are nation builders when they mould today's children as tomorrow's nation builders. They should indeed be the seekers of truth and knowledge, which quality they should pass on to students. They should have an intellectual equipment, ever growing with refined and new knowledge capable of bringing about total development of the students. They should not only provide leadership in the educational field but should also pass on qualities of leadership to each and every student. Here, the advice of Ruskin is note worthy when he says, "education does not mean teaching people to know what they do not know, it means teaching them to behave."

It is imperative that we should broaden the objectives of education, make education a man-making activity and allow it to play an instrumental role in shaping the future of mankind. But this can be achieved only if we restore the glory and greatness of the teaching occupation. Government, people, students and the teachers themselves will have to play an important role in this direction.

The socio-economic ills and other elements prevalent in society, continuous exposure of children to modern electronic media, and the weak and feeble mind of the poor children make entry of educational values in their minds difficult. It is because of this, that the right role of the teacher is very important to give special attention to the weak students. It is here that the parents have to take control of the home environment where the children grow. It is important to know that the greater part of the foundation of the character of the child is laid at home in the very tender age. What takes place in the schools is the perfecting of the foundation already laid at home and building it up further and further.

If the acquired modern behavioural traits are not made inactive that will make the mind of the younger generation insensitive to values and it also dulls their sensitivity to human suffering and pain. Such a condition may lead to slow growth. The individual and the nation will have to pay a heavy price for such a situation. So, the educational action in the mind of such people should help to obtain positive results in this regard. Then only is the total development in the individual possible. There is no denying the fact that the present education allows knowledge to accumulate in the mind of the students but that is only one among the several aspects of educational objectives, all of which, experts say, are needed for the total development of the students, and achieving the goal of a learning society.

In modern times, education should have new and novel technique to overpower and remove hatred, bigotry, fundamentalism, fanaticism, greed and jealousy, narrow outlook and restlessness and other evils prevalent in our society. This is essential to bring out the true objectives of education for the benefit of mankind. In addition to professional and vocational orientation, education should have value-orientation taking into account the erosion of values and deteriorating health and environmental conditions in society. This will give a sense of responsibility along with rights and duties. There should also be an opportunity to every educated individual for employment. Then only will they be able to participate in nation building. Similarly, like vocational education, primary and elementary education should also be made a tool for socio-economic change so that the entire educated people can be partners of growth.

Experts feel that all the educational institutions and learning centres should become temples of learning with its own sanctity, unique quality and rigidity. This will help to achieve the broad objectives of education in a better way for the benefit of mankind. Needless to say the goal of education can be achieved in the desired manner if educationists, experts and teachers play a key role. Research and reforms should be a continuous activity in the field of education as it is imperative to keep pace with the changing times.

There is an imperative need to have a review of our educational system. The purpose of its review will be to re-orient its priorities, make it socially and economically more relevant from the future perspective. In framing a new educational system, the following guidelines contained in the *State of the World Children 2000* published by UNESCO will be a source of inspiration to us, as it is most relevant to the needs of developing countries.

Education systems and programmes must be designed with the best interests of the child and adolescents foremost. Equality and justice, quality of mind and character of the child should be given top priority. They must:

a) Be healthy for children and adolescents;
b) Protect all children and all adolescents;
c) Assure gender equity in access and quality;
d) Involve families and communities;
e) Include family literacy programmes and parent and caregiver education in early childhood care;
f) Be unified and comprehensive, diverse and flexible.;
g) Be efficiently managed and equitably financed;
h) Use both formal and non-formal pedagogies;
i) Assure that all students graduate with the essential skills, knowledge and values to succeed.
j) Use information and communication technologies to reduce disparities in access and quality.

The ability to claim and enjoy the rights of an informed and responsible citizen rests squarely upon a child's access to a good basic education. A quality education—one that encourages children's participation and critical thinking and is infused with the values of peace and human dignity—has the power to transform societies in a single generation. Furthermore, the fulfilment of a child's right to education offers protection from a multitude of hazards, such as a life consigned to poverty, bonded labour in agriculture or industry, domestic labour, commercial sexual exploitation or recruitment to armed conflicts.

For the child's right to education to be fully realised, a strong link must be maintained among service providers in education, health, nutrition, hygiene and sanitation and child protection. The state is accountable and the society is responsible to ensure that the right to education be realised for all children and all adolescents.

The new millennium gives us an opportunity for self-questioning. It would give us a chance to assess our own past contribution to strengthen education and correct ourselves with a view to improve our performance in the sphere of our activity to enrich the life of future man. For instance, if today a teacher asks himself, what is my contribution to achieve the objective of education? What do I do to inculcate values, impart knowledge and develop skill in children? What do I do to update my knowledge ? If all these questions are directed to one's own conscience, the teacher will be able to get interesting answers. It is high time that we resort to such methods to bring out our own potential and strengthen the qualities of our leadership.

Similarly, each student must knock at their life. They should ask, why I am going to school ? What do I do to enrich my knowledge? What do I do to strengthen my character ? Did I respect my teacher? What will be my future ? When my friend is getting a distinction why am I not able to do so?. If they go on questioning their conscience periodically, they will be immensely benefited by it.

In addition to giving knowledge and developing skill, education should generate values, inculcate qualities, and create a learning, refining and purifying spirit so that the mind of the student will be able to keep pace with the changing times with courage and conviction. This will help the children to get an intelligent and self-controlled mind and a working brain. If education deviates from this approach, that will not give any benefit of permanent value to children even if we dump enormous amount of knowledge in their mind through a truck load of textbooks. The mind of a child should be able to absorb good things out of the bulk of knowledge he gets and reject the remains. And what is retained in the mind should be refined to form part of his mind. This is possible only if the mind of the child is endowed with values and qualities to make his mind workable on a continuous basis to carry out the process. So much so, what is important in the education of a child is character building and developing an intelligent mind and a working mind.

What is lacking in the educational sector is not a comprehensive policy, infrastructure, manpower to teach or building to house schools. We have a broadbased education policy and a goal to achieve education for all. Since independence, we have achieved a lot in the area of expansion of educational activities. There are a lot of facilities and infrastructure, though not enough to accommodate all children.

But, surprisingly, what is lacking is harmony and understanding between students themselves, and students and teachers. There is, therefore, a need to create the right atmosphere for education. So, before doing anything more to expand the educational activity, we must set right the atmosphere in the existing institutions. In other words, the sanctity of the temple of learning should be restored. So that the quality of education can be improved for the benefit of the students, nation and mankind as a whole.

What we must understand is that the basic requirement for creating the right atmosphere is harmony. As a learned teacher put it, "Each student is a gift to a school. The teacher should receive and treat them with a smile, with joy and a sense of honour." We should realise that today's children are the citizens of tomorrow and they should be guided and brought up like that. Every student is a genius. The teachers should work hard to bring out their hidden potential and develop in them qualities of leadership, excellence and a spirit to preserve values and culture for their own benefit and for the benefit of future mankind.

In the same way, students must reciprocate the gesture of teachers. They should obey the teachers, respect them and follow them in letter and spirit, for the teachers are their friend, philosopher and guide. So, the first and foremost influential factor in education is the harmony between the students and the teachers. The true goal of education can be achieved only after restoring the crisis of confidence in educational institutions and strengthening harmony. Also we should restore the glory of the teaching profession maintaining a high professional integrity and standard.

Ultimately, education should, *inter alia*, target every human being, keep the floodgates of knowledge wide open without boundaries, foster development, inculcate human values and qualities, awaken talents, empower people, promote friendship and help every individual to live with human dignity through education. Above all, education should always move on the wheels of equality and justice paving the way for a democratic and socialistic spirit in development.

Continuous research and reforms will make educational activity more relevant to current problems and help to remove the ills and weaknesses prevailing in the field of education from time to time. Let us remember that the ultimate goal of a progressive educational system is total development of the individual, a learning society and a global society. Keeping this goal in view, we should have long-term planning in education. In this light, the words of the great Indian scientist Dr. C. V. Raman is an eye-opener to all of us:

> "If you ask me what is the greatest industry of a nation—the key industry. I have no hesitation in saying that it is the production and diffusion of knowledge. There is no nobler work for a man or an Institution than to bring up a young generation in the health and strength and in the vigour of intellectual and physical activity..." "What we lack is perhaps courage, what we lack is perhaps the driving force which takes one anywhere. We have, I think developed an inferiority complex. I think what is needed in India is the destruction of the defeatist spirit. We need a spirit of victory, a spirit that would carry us to our rightful place under the sun, a spirit which will recognise that we, as inheritors of a proud civilisation, are entitled to a rightful place in this planet. If that indomitable spirit were to arise, nothing can hold us from achieving our rightful destiny."

It is that indomitable spirit that we need today to develop a culture of lifelong learning. We should live up to this spirit; lest our society will be far behind that of the growing world.

5

Prevent Population Explosion or Perish

Population growth is slowly going out of control. Population explosion and the associated problems are becoming more and more curious year after year. As a result, environmental degradation has crossed the danger mark endangering the life on earth. The vicious circle of poverty and hunger is enlarging, as development does not move down to the base of the society. Socio- economic ills are increasing posing formidable challenges to mankind. Science and technology is advancing by leaps and bounds, but it does not help to fill the empty stomach of the poor and downtrodden. Even if an aeroplane lands at 'Mars' nothing happens at the base of the society. As the population increases, the base of our society is being overcrowded aggravating the living conditions there. Any further pressure of population will only lead to the collapse of the socio-economic system. At this juncture, the choice before mankind is "Prevent population explosion or Perish." It is high time to open our eyes and make the right choice.

The alarming increase in global population is today the greatest threat to human survival. In spite of the checks and controls exercised by the governments, the global population has reached around six billion with nearly two-thirds of them living in developing and least developed countries. If the 1999 growth rate of 4.1 child per second is allowed to continue, the population will go up in rapid speed. The worst affected will be the developing countries.

The increasing population demands more economic output. The development to meet additional economic output is achieved at the cost of environment. In the case of third world countries, it also increases their global debts to an uncontrollable level. Since the development is not moving to the base of the society, the Socio-economic contradictions there aggravates increasing hunger and misery. The more the population grows, the more the pressure will be at the base of the social structure where a majority of the poor people live.

The unplanned growth of population results in food shortages, malnutrition, illiteracy, diseases, unemployment, violence, indiscipline and other socio-economic problems in developing countries. The alarming increase in these socio-economic ills in our society indicates the devastating effect of population explosion. This indeed is a degenerating trend and in such a situation, human values are bound to be eroded.

There is no denying the fact that mankind is now moving fast to a collapsed stage due to (1) Poverty and hunger, (2) Nuclear proliferation, (3) Increasing debts of third world countries, (4) Huge military expenditure, and (5) Environmental degradation. In view of the serious problems faced by the people of the developing countries, any unplanned growth of population is likely to deepen the present crisis leading to degeneration and self-destruction.

What is important in this context is that if the economic activities and the productivity are below the required level, even the planned population growth will create problems; so much so, what is imperative is full utilisation of available manpower for sustained and equitable development. This is possible only through meticulous planning, decentralised powers of democracy and environment-friendly and poor-friendly development programmes to balance the population with economic growth. It is, therefore, necessary that the population growth is linked to development so that there will be sustained and equitabe growth.

According to statistical information available, there were one million people on earth about 200,000 years ago, 952 million in 1800, 1,000 million in early 19th century, 1,650 million in 1900, 2500 million in 1950, 4,400 million in 1980. The growth between 1950 and 1975 was 2.5 billion to 4 billion. According to projections, the present population of 6 billion is likely to touch 8.3 billion in 2025. The observation of some experts is that a population of more than 10 billion will be unbearable to earth.

There are two ways to look at the control of population. The first one is the theory of the English Priest, T. R. Malthus. According to his theory, "the source and cause of all human suffering is the natural law of absolute over-population, which operates in every age and in every state in which man existed or does now exist. According to his study, the population is presumed to grow at such rates that if not held back by some kind of impediments, it doubles in every 25 years and thus grows in accordance with a geometric progression. Therefore, Malthus concluded that a man who appears on land that is already occupied by other persons does not have any right to require any food for himself, for he is an unwanted person. There is no setting for him at nature's feast. Nature orders him to go away and itself takes measures to ensure that its orders be carried out to check the growth."

The second and most important is the planning done by each country. The growth of population in recent decades indicates that the population control has not been effective in developing countries. There is, therefore, a need to plan meticulously to achieve the desired results in population control. This will reduce the burden of over-population in developing countries which in turn helps to fight poverty and hunger effectively. The developing nations will be able to achieve better economic growth if there is proper control of population.

As already stated, the uncontrolled population leads to a lot of socio-economic problems. It creates a lot of unemployment and also lack of opportunities for people to work. This leads to improper utilisation of manpower to improve productivity. Full utilisation of manpower is necessary for enhancing the income of individuals and providing enough food and other essential commodities to all people. The over-population also increases the problems in the area of materials, fuel, energy, food, environmental pollution, etc.

According to published projections, there will be about a billion hungry person, a billion rural inhabitants, a billion and a half deprived persons who live below the poverty line including a billion extremely poor people, particularly women and children in developing countries in the near future. Another report says 40 per cent of the families in the world share five per cent of the total income.

The magnitude of these problems indicates the adverse effect over-population is having on the living standards of the people. The problem of poverty and hunger is becoming curiouser and curiouser every day. A large number of people are living in slums. At least a few persons there, sometimes, depend on dumping grounds for their livelihood.

The widespread problem of poverty and hunger indicates that there is either a serious shortfall in the production of foodgrains or there is unequal distribution of food articles and the purchasing power of the majority people in the developing countries is extremely low and insufficient. So much so, that increase in food production and its equal distribution avoiding plenty somewhere and scarcity elsewhere, sufficient opportunities for people to work, and contribution of their share to increased productivity and earning a reasonable income, and such other measures are essential to combat poverty and hunger effectively and find appropriate solutions to this important problem of the new age. Better results in this direction can be achieved only if there is proper population control. Peoples and countries of the world should work together to achieve the goal. Global organisations should also join hands with the governments to get clear-cut results in this direction.

In a nutshell, effective control of population will help to stabilise global population and achieve peace and prosperity in the world. Consequently, the goal of a world without fear and hunger can be achieved.

The latest population statistics indicate that life in India will be a struggle of man against man and man against circumstances in the days ahead. This is precisely because we are growing so fast and so large in numbers that mother India will not be able to bear us as honourable citizens or give the essentials of a decent life. Viewed in this light, the future scenario will be unthinkable and the misery of the people untold, if we continue to allow the population to grow at this rate. The matter deserves serious consideration to take constructive steps to reduce the population, which is the one and only way to future peace and prosperity.

Paradoxically, according to the statistics published as on 1 March, 1991 every sixth person in the world is an Indian and every third person in India is under the age of 20. The population of India as on that date was put at 84.39 crores and according to an UN estimate, the population of rest of the world was 443.9 crores, which means 16 per cent of the world population is living in India.

The present global population is estimated at six billion, and one billion people is living in India. The new births between 1981 and 1991 was 160 million in India and the same growth rate has contributed to add another 160 million during 1991 to 2000. Thus, the present estimated population of India is 1,000 million. Thus population statistics put before us a few questions: How are we going to live in the future? Can we give education and employment to the existing 300 million young people? It will be very difficult to find answers to these questions. In such a situation, we can just imagine what would be the fate of the 160 million newborn children in the decade 1991-2000.

In addition to the responsibility of providing food, shelter and other necessities of life to the 1,000 million people, we have a greater and more important responsibility, which obviously concerns our future, the future of mankind. We have today with us about 320 million children below the age of 20 years. This tender segment of our population should be educated, disciplined and trained as future nation builders in the next 20 years. This indeed is a herculean task. This is precisely because we do not know how much children we can accommodate in our educational institutions. We do not know how much more food our land can produce.

We do not know as to how many more houses and shelters can be built for these future citizens. We do not know what type of natural calamities await us as a result of destruction of natural wealth and pollution of air, land and water. And in such an unplanned manner, the result will be degeneration and destruction. It will be a case of self-destruction of an age-old culture through increasing inertia, indiscipline, violence, poverty, pollution, misery and selfishness.

Experts feel that a substantial reduction in new births will help the government to set clearcut and achievable goals to improve the quality of life of the people and speed up the socio-economic growth. Economic growth of a nation would depend upon the full utilisation of available manpower, less number of idle and depending population, balanced growth of population and employment opportunities and transfer of technology to rural areas. In this direction, the following factors are important to link population growth with development:

1. Balanced growth of working population and depending population.
2. Full utilisation of land available to increase productivity.
3. Industrialisation in line with the developments in the developed world.
4. Full cooperation between and active involvement of the government, non-governmental organisations and community to implement the population control programme linked to total development.
5. Rigid social audit to ensure that the beneficiary is getting the full money spent by the government, and there is permanent socio-economic upliftment in each family.

Economic development requires greater investment in agriculture, industry, public health, education and such other vital areas of development. Population explosion results in high percentage of depending population and less working population. It increases the burden on education and public health services. It increases the pressure on land and undermines the health and ability of people to work. All these factors slow down the growth of national income, gross national product and gross domestic product. Thus high population growth holds back economic and social development. Hunger and malnutrition—a major problem of the third world countries—is the result of over-population and low productivity. If the new birth rates are reduced that will pave the way for the smooth implementation of the economic programmes of the country.

Population and Poverty

Surprisingly and understandably, poverty is a curse in developing countries. In these countries, the majority of the people—the working people, the village people, the poor people and the weaker sections—are victims of poverty and misery. In India, according to official reports, about 30 per cent of the population are living below the poverty line. Anyhow, poverty is widely prevalent in India, particularly in rural areas. Private studies estimate that about 42.7 per cent of the population is living below the poverty line. It is common knowledge that over-population is the root cause of India's poverty and misery. Obviously, the nation has to feed, clothe and house people, whose number is far ahead of its capacity to do so.

It is therefore essential that the population growth be controlled in a planned manner in accordance with the capacity of the nation to provide them the necessities of daily life. We must understand the economic, social and political dangers of the world's failure to control its population growth. Democracy cannot survive unless the standard of living of the backward countries of the world is substantially improved. This is an impossible task in the prevailing circumstances.

Over-population is the result of high birth rate, which reduces the saving and per capita income. High birth rate means high percentage of dependent children. In India we had about 160 million children aged between 10 and 20 born between 1981 and 1991 and another 160 million aged below 10 born between 1991 and 2000. So, poor families with high birth rate are forced to live in a hand-to-mouth situation, as the income is insufficient to meet the requirements of the family. What is true of a family is equally true of the collection of families, which constitute a nation.

The income in such families, insufficient to meet even the requirement of one or two children, are shared by more children. As a result of this, there is inadequacy of food, clothing and other necessities of life in most of the families in rural India. Over and above, the parents are not able to educate and guide their children properly. This creates a lot of problems in the attitude and behaviour of children which ultimately leads to a series of social problems. These children are often misguided and their future spoiled by circumstances.

The crowded home is responsible for all these undesirable social orders in the family. A crowded home is always unhygenic and unhappy due to over-population. The home and surroundings of such people become breeding centres for the virus of various diseases.

Unless and until the number of children is brought down in each family through effective population control, we cannot remove poverty from India. We will not be able to improve the quality of life of the large number of people affected by poverty. There is no shortcut to escape from poverty, except gainful employment and hard work. This can be achieved only if there is a balanced growth of population. Population control should begin from each family. This is the only way to increase productivity and per capita income, and to rescue the poverty-stricken people from hunger and misery.

According to reports, the total working population in India is only about 33.4 per cent. This clearly indicates that such a small percentage of working population can never take the nation forward, particularly when the population is growing in an unplanned manner among the majority rural people. There is no scope for gainful employment to the newcomers, as we have already millions of unemployed people with us, and on a first-come-first-serve basis, they should be given an opportunity to work. Unless we put to work at least 90 per cent of the healthy adult population and increase agricultural and industrial production substantially, we cannot increase the per capita income of the people as a prelude to improve the standard of living and quality of life.

It is an acknowledged fact that India has made far-reaching achievements in the field of industry and agriculture since independence, but the poverty still exists. This is precisely because the demand is more than what is produced, and what is produced is far below the actual requirement and consequently there is always a short supply of food and other articles.

According to experts, poverty is eating the life of the poor people. A majority of the poor people in rural areas have no choice of food, clothes or shelter. A majority of the people in rural areas, particularly women and children, are victims of malnutrition, which makes their body a breeding centre for diseases. Shortage of food, vitamins and proteins results in a living environment below human dignity. Inadequacy of food condemns thousands of our mothers and children in rural areas to permanent ill-health and disability.

According to experts, the minimum needs of daily diet like cereals, milk, pulses, leafy and non-leafy vegetables, fruits, oils, etc., is not within the reach of common man. An average Indian diet is far below this requirement and a large number of people can never think of such a full-fledged diet in their life. It can be seen that rural people are facing serious problem of malnutrition. With the increase in the prices of essential commodities far in excess of the purchasing power of the common man, they have no access to the required minimum food items.

So, the malnutritional problem is a deep-rooted malice among the poverty-sticken and rural people, and it is very difficult to uproot it. Every individual has to give a hand to uproot this malice and save the people from poverty and misery, and this can be achieved only by rigid population control.

In this light, it can be seen that we cannot remove poverty and raise the majority people suffering from poverty, unless we control our population and bring it down to the least possible level. The problems of over-population are complicating all other problems in the country and widening the vicious circle of poverty.

India has vast untapped human potential. Perhaps only a small percentage of the available potential is being developed and used now. We should have facilities to develop the human potential further and to use it for various purposes, like increasing productivity and national income etc. This can be achieved only if there are opportunities to work. There is a need for meticulous planning to find employment to the existing population, and the success of this plan would depend upon the control of population. To meet the increasing human wants, we are also exploiting the natural wealth, like forests, which will soon disappear if we continue the present method of destructions on earth. In order to prevent such a situation, we should refrain from destroying the forests. As a first step in this direction, we should control our population.

According to reports, if Indian population grows at the rate of 2.5 per cent per annum, i.e., less than the present rate of growth, resources requirement for this addition would be:

12,565,300	quintals of food
188,774,000	metres of cloth
2,509,000	houses
126,500	schools
372,500	school teachers
4	million jobs

It is clear that the existing food production and other essential commodities are insufficient to meet the require-ments of the present population. This can be seen when we look at the 30 per cent of the total population living below the poverty line. When a good number of people, particularly in rural areas and slums, are not assured of one-time meal, clothes to change, the ability to read and write, shelter to protect them from rain and sun, and justice against exploitation, we can very well imagine the difficulties in providing daily necessities of life like food, cloth, education and other requirements and job opportunities to the 16 million people being added every year. This would mean that the new population will only fall into the vicious circle of poverty, misery and hardship. This can be prevented only by balancing the population control and productivity.

6

Family Planning: Future Challenges and Commitments

> In developing countries like India, where population explosion is a stumbling-block to sustained and equitable development, family planning is the one and only way to achieve progress. In our society, where the majority of the people are victims of poverty, hunger, exploitation, diseases, violence and social chaos, the two-child norm is indispensable to achieve the socialistic goals of democracy. We should accept the two-child norm as a patriotic and constitutional duty. Every citizen and the community as a whole should be responsible and accountable in the matter of family planning. Our indifference and callous attitude, if not changed, will only lead to the collapse of the socio-economic system and consequently our democratic set up. It is high time that we realise the seriousness of the problem and rededicate ourselves to work for the success of the population control programmes.

Equality and justice in the matter of development, and peace and progress of the future society would depend upon the seriousness with which we implement the family planning programmes. There is a need to make it a patriotic and constitutional duty making every citizen and the community responsible and accountable.

In a nutshell, the future family planning programme should be a movement of the people. The planning of the family should begin from the grass root level and each family should be considered as a basic unit. The family planning slogan should move into the minds of the people making them understand that its purpose is to help the individual, the family and the nation to survive and prosper.

"The effect of today's population trends will be felt in the years to come. Measures aimed at modifying the trends will be felt by future generations. It is the future generation who reap the benefits or pay the price for our action or inaction today." These words of an eminent writer should be our guiding philosophy. While discussing about family planning, we are reminded of the thought-provoking words of our former Prime Minister Indira Gandhi, while accepting the UN Population Award at New York on 30 September 1983: "I see population planning, as indeed any other programme, not in terms of number but in terms of individuals, men, women and children, and of human realities. Every child, said Rabindranath Tagore, is a reminder that God has not despaired of man. But so many million children in the world are victims of human despair and poverty. They are denied rightful share of food, shelter, learning and love. Child bearing should be a joy, not a burden, and since it is the mother who bears and rears the child, we are concerned not only with her health but her will. Family planning is a proof of our love for children and a test of our claim to be a good mother, a good father and a good society."

The living conditions of the majority people in rural areas, the unplanned urban growth, environmental damages, impending food crises, illiterate women and girls, malnutrition of majority rural women and children, extent of infant and maternal mortality, low status of women in society, and growing indiscipline and violence both in the family and the society, call for immediate action to enforce the family planning in each and every family. There is need for a change in the attitude and outlook of the people in this direction.

In this connection, an observation in the *State of the World Population Report* of the UN Population Fund is an inspiring piece to us: "Family Planning is far more than merely contraception. It is part of an environment in which everyone has opportunities and choices. Building these opportunities begins at birth, and depends among other things on the position of girls and women in their society. Higher status for women brings more ability to choose, where the choice is available, women will take advantage of it." The report further adds: "The experience of the last 20 years shows that strong well-managed family planning programmes are highly effective. By purely voluntary means, they have achieved smaller family size, healthier mothers and children, and more balanced rates of population growth in developing countries in many different parts of the world, and in a wide variety of social and economic setting."

Family planning should be linked to the total development programmes of the nation. Population is not just a control programme. It is a question of planning the life of every individual, every family and every nation. This is essential to combine the population control; and the improvement of the standard of living of the people and the elimination of poverty, misery, ignorance, pollution, overcrowding, diseases and idleness.

In order to achieve the above goal of total development, the planning should take into account the following aspects:

1. Importance of the views and attitude of the individual.
2. Removing prejudices and misunderstanding from the minds of the people.
3. Option to limit the family by convenient methods.
4. Gainful employment to all adults in the family.
5. Pure drinking water and better living environment.
6. All-round development of the locality.
7. Making health services and food supply within easy reach of all the people.

The status of women, their welfare, health, education and development are crucial factors in achieving success in the total development of the family. Fertility control needs the participation of millions of women, and as a matter of policy, this should be voluntary. Education should inculcate attitudinal changes and behavioural changes in couples to achieve positive results.

The broad objectives of a National Family Planning Programme should give weightage to the views of the community. All relevant information about the family planning should be made available to the families in rural areas through various contact programmes and communication. Family planning is an input for development. Social change and prosperity and a comfortable life will not come to a family where there are a large number of children and a lot of connected social problems.

The fact that the population of India has reached about 1,000 million in the year 2000 in spite of the top priority given to the population control in our National Plan reveals the population trends and the additional efforts and changes needed to achieve the goal aimed at. During the past few decades, the emphasis of the family planning was mainly on supply of contraceptives and sterilisation. The present growth trend has revealed that the existing method, measures and activities of population control are not effective in the sense that it has not brought the expected results. We have to go miles to achieve our real goal. It has not taken into account vital aspects such as the living conditions of the people, health and development of women, involvement of the community, adequate family counselling and post-medical services, etc., which are essential for the overall improvement in the standard of life. This can be achieved only if we link the population programme to total development.

In this light, the message of the Prime Minister of India on World Population Day—11 July 1991—is a thought-provoking one: "The World Population Day focuses on a subject which is of global concern and of particular importance to a country like ours engaged in a struggle to eradicate poverty and improve the quality of life of our people. This is an occasion for us to redouble our efforts to create population consciousness, attain a more acceptable rate of population growth and create conditions which will help utilise the full potential of our population as a development resource.

The problems of allocating our scarce resources to particular demands has been further compounded by our fast growing population. The rate at which our population is expanding has prevented the full benefits of economic development from reaching our people, particularly the weaker sections. Vast numbers have to do without the basic amenities of life and other facilities which would have enabled them to live fuller lives. This has also affected adversely our efforts to utilise the full potential of our people for the development process.

Government is committed to creating conditions for improving the quality of life of our millions and will accord high priority in dealing with the problem of population. While government will do its utmost, the role of non-governmental organisations and individual volunteers in creating population consciousness among the people is of tremendous importance. Concerted efforts are needed to take the message of population consciousness to the remotest of remote areas. Our people must be made fully conscious of the fact that their own future depends upon the success of the population control programme. They must realise that it is the small family which holds the key to their prosperity and well being tremendous."

The following suggestions may be useful in achieving the family planning objectives.

Education

All educational activities in the country, irrespective of its nature and level, should have an appropriate coverage of the population control education. Inculcation of population consciousness and a feeling of brotherhood in the age young will help a lot in developing a positive attitude and outlook in the younger generation about population control. In addition to the specific programmes in schools, colleges and universities, there should be textbook level teaching in schools and colleges so that correct and complete knowledge about the population growth can be given to the younger generation.

Population Control Zones

The entire country should be divided into population zones depending upon the rate of population growth in each area. There should be special efforts and programmes to cover the people in the zone where the population growth is very high. Family planning should be made part of the development programmes in each zone. This will help to identify the target group easily and to understand their needs in its proper perspective.

Promotional Role

Employers, rich people, and the elite of the society have to play an instrumental role in promoting family planning. Employers should make all efforts to make their employees accept the concept of small family through various programmes and incentives. Similarly, the educated people, the elite in the society and the well-to-do can also contribute significantly in promoting family planning.

Media

The media has to play a vital role in promoting family planning. They should give some sort of publicity on their own on a daily basis. This will help to make the information within the reach of all sections of the society. The role of TV, radio and cinema is also very important as any message conveyed through these channels will land in the minds of the people in an effective way.

Religious and Political Sanctions

It is a known fact that some times political thoughts and religious philosophy keeps the people away from the population control. Religious pandits and political leaders will have to play a crucial role in removing this hurdle, which is essential to save mankind from degeneration and destruction. If the religions and political organisations are for the welfare and well-being of mankind, then the population control should be an important agenda for them. There should not be any political or religious hurdle in promoting family planning. In other words, family planning should have political and religious sanctions so that people can avail the facilities for their own welfare and progress.

A Package Deal

Family planning programmes should be made a package deal linked to food supply, immunisation, water supply, housing and sanitation, employment, health and medical services and such other facilities of life. This will help to achieve better results both in population control and development.

Leadership

The management of the family planning programme is very important. The sincerity, dedication and efforts put in this direction will bring positive results only if there is dynamic and efficient management. Leadership at all levels right from the family level to the national level is an indispensable factor for providing better management of family planning. There should also be an audit machinery exclusively for family planning to ascertain whether the money allotted is reaching the beneficiary and whether the plans and programmes are implemented as envisaged by the government. Issue of free health cards for treatment in government hospitals and free ration cards to people living below the poverty line can also be considered, as this will bring good results in reducing the births in rural areas.

Population explosion, environmental degradation, over-exploitation of natural resources and a host of related factors are threatening life on earth as never before. India is the grimmest example of all. There are millions of unemployed, and one-third of the population has insufficient income. Poverty, violence, social chaos and indiscipline grow faster than the development.

In order to remove the above situation, population control should be made a patriotic, mandatory and constitutional duty of every citizen. The government should implement a practicable policy to implement the two-child norm. The policy may *inter alia*, consider the following norms.

1. Two-child norm should be mandatory for contesting elections to all public offices.
2. Two-child norm should be made compulsory along with qualification and age to all future appointments in central government, state government, banks, local bodies, public sector undertakings and autonomous Institutions.
3. Two-child norm should also be introduced for higher education, scholarship, government-level concessions and others facilities.
4. Other incentives and schemes should be provided to promote two-child norm among the people.

The success of the population control would depend, to a large extent, upon the following factors:

1. Importance and priorities given in the National Plan for population control.
2. Linking of population control to total development programmes.

3. Understanding of the problems by the people and a positive change in their attitude and outlook.
4. Providing right information to all the people.
5. Education, development and freedom of women.
6. Availability of convenient methods and choices for family planning.
7. Availability of health and medical services locally.
8. Frequent monitoring to assess the progress.
9. Participation and involvement of individual volunteers, non-governmental organisations and the community.
10. Incentives and benefits after adopting the small family concept for overall improvement of quality of life. Assured employment to all families adopting the two child norm.
11. Religious and political sanctions.
12. Competent personnel with expertise and technical skill to provide family planning service and counselling.
13. A follow-up mechanism which promotes a continuity of contraceptive use.
14. Services are convenient and easily accessible to all sections of the population and should also meet their existing health needs.
15. Reliability of services, counselling and referral systems wherever necessary.
16. An integrated health services.

In view of the vast difference in the social and cultural aspects of the people, and the varying rates of population growth in different parts of the country, such as high birth areas, low birth areas, etc., there is a need for area specific projects with a lot of incentives and packages.

There is, therefore, need for a lot of decentralisation in the implementation of population control programmes so that awareness and motivation are created by the local community. This will make the family planning programmes a people-oriented one. Needless to say, panchayati raj institutions should be entrusted with the responsibility of population control.

Since human survival is being questioned by over-population, it is high time for us to move fast, individually and collectively, with dedication and sincerity towards the goal of population control and total development. That will help to regulate the growth of new population, develop and utilise the existing human potential for development, and mould the children of today as talented nation builders of tomorrow.

7

Importance of Character in Future Society

The character of a nation is a reflection of the character of its people, and the character of the people today is the character of the children of yesterdays. The behaviour, attitude and outlook of the people is a true reflection of their character. The peace and prosperity of the future society depends, to a great extent, on the character of its people. Here, the golden words of Martin Luther will serve as an eye-opener to us: "The prosperity of a country depends not on the abundance of its revenue, not on the strength of its fortification, not on the beauty of its public buildings, but it consists in the number of its cultivated citizens, in its men of education, enlightenment and character." So much so, character is of supreme importance in building a nation. Unfortunately, a serious crises in human character is evident in our present day society. As a result, there is erosion of values and degeneration in every sphere of activity. Indiscipline, negative and rebellious attitude and selfishness is widely prevalent, endangering future prosperity. If this trends is allowed to continue, it may lead to self-destruction. We must remember that the future growth and survival would depend upon the strong character of today's children. This should be our vision for the 21st century. We should strive hard to lay a strong foundation of character in the minds of our children and shape our vision into reality.

Character is the sum total of many human values and virtues. So, education should generate essential values which forms the basic foundation of good, strong and undeterred character.

Character is a precious gift of education. Without character, education, health and social status are of no avail. It helps to stabilise qualities like discipline, self-control, patience, social consciousness, brotherhood, tolerance and courage. The effort to form a solid foundation of character in children should begin at home in early childhood and parents have an important role to play in this regard. The importance of character should be restored in education and then only can we achieve the true goal of education. If we fail to lay a strong foundation of character in children even the pyramids of knowledge we build in their mind later may become obsolete. Education, experts say, is a way of learning to think, learning to understand, learning to know, learning to respect, learning to behave, learning to distinguish good and bad, and learning to do things in the right perspective in all fields of human activity. This goal can be achieved only if we lay the foundation for a strong character and positive thinking in children.

Paradoxically, we are now on the verge of collapse of our character. The indecent manners, violent behaviour, social disorders and selfishness, corruption, indifference and callous attitude are the symptoms of this crisis. The crisis in character is due to degeneration of moral and social values. The increasing social problems, conflicts and confrontation are an indication that we are in the midst of a crisis. The truth in the good old saying "When wealth is lost, nothing is lost, when health is lost something is lost, and when character is lost, everything is lost" is slowly coming to light.

Today, the intellectual, moral, cultural, social and other important qualities are in danger. The result will be a serious crisis in character. The unending struggle between man and man, man and environment and man and circumstances is deepening the crisis in character.

Understandably, we see that the quality of man is slowly losing its image in our society. There are symptoms of it in our society and some of them are lack of respect to parents, elders, teachers, women and children and lack of knowledge; growing indiscipline, destructive tendencies, disobedience and other negative qualities. This is a very sad state of affairs which if allowed to continue will lead to degeneration of human values and culture.

We must understand that in the life of an individual, character is most important. Similarly, in the life and growth of nation, character is of utmost importance. Character is the supreme of all assets. The great wisdom of character can be seen in the words of Martin Luther: "The prosperity of a country depends not on the abundance of its revenue, not on the strength of its fortification, not on the beauty of its public buildings, but it consists in the number of its cultivated citizens, in its men of education, enlightenment and character."

The character is the noblest of all possessions of man. It reflects in every manner, every action, every thought, every feeling, every habit and every behaviour of man. So, a crisis in character means, a crisis in all these qualities of man. Our duty would be to prevent a crisis in character and to strengthen it further to meet the future challenges.

Swami Vivekananda said, "Education is a man-making process." The basis for this man-making process is good character laid at home in childhood. Home is the best and most important school of character.

Eminent people say, it is in the home where habits are formed, where intellect awakened, where character moulded for good or bad. It is here that the foundation for qualities like discipline, patience, understanding, broadmindedness, self-control, self-confidence, obedience and other moral values are laid.

As children grow up, they should acquire all qualities needed for a good character. They should grow as obedient, hardworking, honest, and disciplined citizen. This way only can we prevent a crisis or a deterioration in the character of future citizens. This way only, can we prevent the decay of our civilisation.

So, we should help the children of today to develop a good character. Remember, character is the best of all human possessions. We must prevent a crisis in character at all costs. This is essential to make our life healthy. Good character helps to prevent diseases and enrich our life.

It is, therefore, imperative to protect this noble quality and virtue of man. Going deep into the character-building process in human beings, we see that the women who are the managers of home environment have to play a key role in moulding children with good character.

In this context, there is a great relevance in the words of Gandhiji: "Education of man is the education of individual and the education of women is the education of the family." Home is the first and most important school of character. It is there that every human being receives his best moral training, for it is there that he inherits those principles which endure through life. Home training includes manners and character building. It is at home where habits are formed, intellect awakened, and character moulded for good or bad. The home is regarded as the most potential and influential school of civilisation, for it is the character and habits formed there that form the foundation of a civilisation.

The homes where the spirit of love and duty prevades, where the daily life is honest and virtuous, where the governance is sensible, wise, kind, and disciplined such home is a fertile land for character building. The child cannot help imitating what he sees. Everything to him is a model, of manner, of gesture, of speech, of habit and character. Obviously, the model before every child's eye is his mother. The good mother, said George Herbert, "is worth a hundred school masters. In the home, she is the loadstone to all hearts and loadstar to all eyes."

It is because the mother influences the action and conduct of the child, that her good example is of so much importance in home. She is the example and model constantly before their eyes whom children unconsciously observe and imitate. The maternal love is the visible providence of our race. Women cultivate in children habits and feelings, which determine their behaviour and character. Home is the true school of courtesy, of which woman is always the best instructor. The good home is thus the best of schools.

Napoleon was accustomed to say that the future good or bad conduct of a child depended entirely on mother. He himself attributed his rise in life in a great measure to the training of his will by his mother. One of the most charming features in the character of Samuel Johnson was the tenderness with which he invariably spoke of his mother—a woman of strong understanding who firmly implanted in his mind, as he himself acknowledged, his first impressions of religion.

Thus, it can be seen that the role of mothers in home environment is the determining factor in the shaping of character and ability of their children. There is, therefore, a need to give due importance to this role not only in society but also in the education of women. Perhaps the crisis we are witnessing now in the character of the younger generation may be due to the insignificant and ineffective role played by the women in moulding their children.

The reason for the insignificant role of women in this direction can be attributed to (a) lack of quality education—majority of them illiterates, (b) socio-economic problems at home, (c) cultural prejudices and social inhibitions against women which still give a lower status to them in the family (d) large number of children in the family making it difficult to attend to them individually, (e) non-recognition of their active role in character building, and (f) overwork leaving little time for proper home management.

However, to save the younger generation from degeneration, there is an imperative need to inculcate in them a new spirit through good character and behaviour. Effort in this direction has to begin at home, and mothers have to shoulder this responsibility. The observation in the *State of World Children 2000* is worth emulating:

> Education does not begir when the child sets foot in the primary school, nor does it end when the school bell rings and class lets out. Learning begins at birth, it occurs in

> the family, in communities, during play. Life's teachers are parents, siblings, peers, workplaces, the mass media.

When a mother asked a clergyman when she should begin the education of the child, then four years old, he replied, "Madam, if you have not begun already, you have lost those four years. From the first smile that gleams upon an infant's cheek, your opportunity begins."

Let us remember the words of Lord Brougham who observed that between the ages of eighteen and thirty months, a child learns more of the material world, of his own powers, of the nature of other bodies and even of his own mind and other minds, than he acquires during all the rest of his life.

There is need for a change in the home environment to help good character formation in children in early childhood. The educational institutions should also help to strengthen the character of the children and adolescents. The social behaviour in society should serve as a model to character building in children. The programmes in the fast developing electronic media should help children to strengthen their character. Children should be helped to keep away from programmes which are likely to weaken their character and cripple their behaviour. The parents, teachers, elders and the community as a whole should create a favourable environment to develop a strong character as a basic foundation in the mind of children. In such a foundation only can they build discipline and self-control as pillars of their mind. We must remember that safety, security and growth are not possible without these qualities, So, the nation should be concerned about the deteriorating character in our society, which, if allowed to continue, may lead to degeneration and self-destruction. We have before us the lessons from the fallen individuals, disintegrated families and perished civilisations. We should learn from the past and work hard to save the people from the present crisis in character. Whether it is an individual, a family, an organisation, or a nation, a strong character is of paramount importance. The people, the nation and the society should not forget this truth, as the future peace and prosperity depends on this truth.

8

Education, Panchayati Raj and Democracy

> We are witnessing a sea-change in the global economy as a result of globalisation in different countries. As a result, the global economy, and even the national economy of several countries, are growing but the poor man's economy the world over is going down. The socio-economic contradictions within the people of developing countries are widening year after year. This situation prevails even in developing nations which are endowed with rich resources, human potential and materials. In view of this one-sided growth, the majority of the population of the world living in the developing world are victims of poverty, malnutrition, exploitation, illiteracy, inequality and injustice and discrimination. When there is surplus food at the upper layer of the society, the story of increasing scarcity and hunger is heard at the base of the social structure. At times, at least a few people are forced to depend on dumping grounds for their livelihood. It seems that the socio-economic change in human society has affected only a small percentage of women and a large number of them are today victims of poverty, malnutrition, unemployment, sexual exploitation and discrimination, social instability and prejudices. In any democracy, each and every man and woman should have access to knowledge, health, educational opportunities, economic opportunities, civil liberties and rights, and empowerment. Education and panchayati raj are the only way to open up the mind of the poor people for change and progress.

The development curve should slope down towards the base of the society. This is possible only if we enforce a socialistic and democratic spirit in our development programmes. Education and panchayati raj are the two wheels to move in this direction. Protection, education, empowerment and employment are our main objectives. To achieve this goal, our priority should be education and panchayati raj.

The end of fifty years of Indian Republic is the beginning of the new millennium. This indeed was a great event. It is a glorious occasion for a retrospection. In doing so, we can be proud of the tremendous progress made by our country during the second half of the 20th century. Such an effort will also reveal the imperative need to enforce a democratic and socialistic spirit in our development in order to give a better deal for the unempowered, voiceless and weaker sections of the society. This is to extend the facilities and benefits of democracy and development, now available to the upper half of the population, to the other and lower half also, who are unable to go nowhere near the development taking place in the changing world. In other words, it gives an opportunity for all of us to undertake a self-questioning exercise and conduct an honest social audit of our conscience. In this regard, let us remember the famous saying of Philip James: "The highest among the court of justice is the court of conscience." In this process let us ask, what do I do as a citizen to uphold the democratic and socialistic spirit of the Constitution? What do I do for the unfortunate and poor people? And what do we, as Indians, do to take all people with us in our march towards progress and peace? Such an honest social audit of our conscience would reveal that at least half of our own countrymen, with the same rights and privileges like us, are living in the hot furnace of poverty, misery, exploitation, illiteracy, ignorance and discrimination. They are the poor, poverty-stricken, and downtrodden who are trapped at the bottom of the society.

The plight and the living conditions of a sizable female population is very pathetic and deplorable. It appears that the majority of them are nowhere near having the rights and privileges available to them both in our Constitution and democracy. Our insensitiveness and callous attitude to female half of the population is a matter of concern to the lovers of democracy, the *raison d'etre* of which lies in the socialistic principles of equality and justice.

Gender inequality, dowry deaths, atrocities and crimes, home violence, poverty and malnutrition, diseases, sexual exploitation and prejudice are the major problems invading the life of women. Education, social, economic and political empowerment, protection from violence and crimes and gender equality, are indispensable to utilise the energies of women, who constitute half of the population of the country, for the revitalisation of development and democratic process in line with the socialistic goals of our democracy.

An honest social audit would further reveal that only a section of the population enjoys over-consumption and gets the benefits of the consumption explosion in abundance. In spite of the green revolution and self-reliance in food production, millions of people are not getting essential food articles and are struggling for existence. When half of the people drink pure water, beer and cool drinks, the other half drinks unsafe water and live in unhygenic conditions. And above all, when a large section of the upper and middle class takes home a lion's share of the government exchequer, and when the banks write off tens of crores of rupees, the majority poor people do not have the money to buy the essentials. Some feast while others starve, and uneven development is now the base of our democracy. Existence of plenty for some people and poverty for others, wasteful consumption of the rich, non-availability of even that waste to the extremely poor, change in some areas and stagnation in other areas are explicitly clear in our society.

In this connection, the observation in the *Human Development Report 1998*, would be an eye-opener to us. It reads: "The poorest 20 per cent of the world's people and more have been left out of the consumption explosion. Well over a billion people are deprived of the basic consumption needs. Of the 4.4 billion people in developing countries, nearly three-fifths lack basic sanitation. Almost a third have no access to clean water. A quarter do not attend school to grade 5. About a fifth do not have enough dietary energy and protein. Micro-nutrient deficiencies are even more widespread. Worldwide, two billion people are anemic, including 55 million in industrial countries. In developing countries only a privileged minority has motorised transport, telecommunications and modern energy."

And now let us ask ourselves, Are we, as a people and a society, heading for a breakdown? If we are able to give all facilities and benefits of democracy and development to a section of the people living at the upper and middle layer of the society, that too, with an overdose of equality and justice, why have we failed to extend the same benefits, privileges and facilities to the majority people living at the base of the society? What prevented us from providing the base necessities of a decent life to these unfortunate people, whose rights and privileges are in no way inferior to others? We are duty bound to give them all the facilities for keeping up the dignity and decency of human life.

Now the task before us is to work on a war-footing to upgrade the living status of the poor people. Economic development has been the watchword in India's march into the 21st century. Paradoxically development has sidelined the majority rural people and slum-dwellers resulting in a lot of economic contradictions and inequality. There is no disputing the fact that our development has been, to a large extent, at the cost of the poor and downtrodden and environment. And in India the cost of ecological devastation, pollution-caused health problems and environment damage is estimated at 13.8 billion dollars a year. There is, therefore, an imperative need to change the development strategy to make it environment—friendly and poor-friendly. The development goals and priorities should slope down towards the base of the society, where the majority poor people live in deplorable and miserable conditions. Then only, can we march forward as one people, one society in a democratic and socialistic spirit.

But there is no magic to achieve this goal. The one and the only way to bring development at the lower strata of the society is panchayati raj. In other words, planning and its implementation with honesty and total dedication will alone bring prosperity and peace at the base of the Indian society.

Panchayati raj, as a three-tier system of governance of villages at gram, block and district level, brings the powers of democracy at the hands of the people making it a real "Government of the people, by the people and for the people." Nearly 70 per cent of our people are living in villages and as such the progress of the nation would, by and large, depend upon the development of rural areas. The development of rural areas would depend upon the increased decentralisation of power, effectiveness and efficiency of the panchayati raj system and the honest implementation of the plans and programmes to obtain positive results.

Relevant here are the words of the first Prime Minister of India, Jawaharlal Nehru: "Over 80 per cent of our people live in villages. India is poor because the villages of India are poor. India will be rich if the villages of India are rich. Therefore, the basic problem of India is to remove the poverty from the Indian villages. Some years ago, we abolished Zamindari and Jagirdari systems in various parts of India, because the villages of India could not prosper under semi-feudal system of land ownership. This is not enough, we have to go ahead further. Panchayat should be given greater power. For, we want the villager to have a measure of real swaraj in his own village. He should have power and not have to refer everything to big officials. We do not want the official to interfere too much in the life of the villager. We want to build swaraj right from the village up."

The responsibility of the panchayati raj institutions is and will always be to make people accountable for development, and the development should give them real benefits for permanent socio-economic progress. The over-all socio-economic development would mean significant improvement in all aspects of life including traditional vocations, agricultural production, electricity power, irrigation and water supply, transport, banking, credit facilities, health and sanitation.

These and many other tasks and responsibilities can be carried out by the people only if they get proper education and empowerment. So, education should prepare people to take up responsibilities of nation building. Educational emancipation of people is indispensable to expedite economic development. Thus, education for all should be a priority goal of any nation to achieve the desired results in development. This goal should be entrusted with the panchayati raj institutions.

The panchayati raj has to target every individual and family to solve the social, economic, health, employment and other problems of the people at the grassroots level and bring about overall development. This can be achieved only if education gives them knowledge, talents, intelligence, leaderships qualities and character. Such an education alone will be able to empower the people to carry out their socio-economic responsibilities in a democratic spirit. It is therefore, essential that the right type of education should move into the mind of man to meet the challenges of the changing times.

Keeping in view the requirement and objectives, it can be said that education is a tool for socio-economic change. In a nutshell, education of the rural people should have the following broad objectives to achieve the goal set by the panchayat raj.

a) To create the whole gamut of skills—manual, technical, clerical, executive, managerial, and others—which are essential to carry out development in rural areas.
b) To improve the existing traditional vocations in rural areas like agricultural work, weavers of cloth, potters, blacksmith, carpenters, oil crushers, artists and so on.
c) To improve productivity in all sectors of the economy.
d) To utilise the advance of science and technology to improve the living standards of rural people and to accelerate development.
e) To create a spirit for voluntary action and team work among the people.

f) To provide health education to create awareness about causes of diseases, prevention of diseases, problems of malnutrition, cleanliness and hygiene and such other vital information.

We must make education a responsibility, and a commitment of the government, panchayati raj institutions, non-governmental organisation, families, communities and citizens. Then and then alone, can we achieve the goal aimed at. In other words, education of rural people is a means to an end, the end being total development aimed at by panchayati raj.

Panchayati raj has to go miles and miles to cover the illiterate and semi-literate rural people through a result-oriented educational movement and empower them to shoulder the responsibility entrusted to them. Had the rural people been socially conscious, alert, educated and capable, it would have been possible to achieve tremendous progress through panchayati raj and join the mainstream of nation building.

We are unable to reach the goal of panchayati raj due to various factors such as illiteracy, backwardness, lack of social consciousness and a socialistic spirit, absence of honesty and total dedication, inequality and injustice. Education should be geared up to change this unfavourable environment and train people to provide honest, effective and efficient leadership in the implementation of people's planning. Education is, therefore, a connecting link between the rural people, and development. The vision of Gandhiji on panchayati raj is also an important message for us. Gandhiji said: "Independence must begin at the bottom. Thus every village will be a republic or panchayat having full powers. It follows, therefore, that every village has to be self-sustained and capable of managing its affairs." Needless to mention that we can achieve the goal set by the Father of the Nation only through a result-oriented, value-generating and job-oriented education in villages.

Total development is the ultimate goal of the panchayati raj. It means total development of every family and every community in a society. But this is possible only if education makes every person in society honest, dynamic and dedicated worker. Then only will the benefits of development move into the socio-economic fabric of rural life bringing about far-reaching changes to keep pace with the changing times. Thus, education should make peoples' participation an accelerator of socio-economic transformation of rural people. In other words, education is the key instrument to change the rural economy.

We celebrate 50 years of our republic and yet approximately five out of ten people in India are still illiterate, seven out of ten women are illiterate, eight out of ten tribals are illiterate and eight out of ten scheduled castes are illiterates. It is, therefore, clear that the panchayati raj will succeed in building up the village economy only if people are liberated from illiteracy. When people are educated modern science and technology will move uninterruptedly into rural areas accelerating the pace of development. Education also drives away superstition, prejudice, dogma, selfishness, idleness and insensitiveness to human problems and paves the way for flow of science and technology to speed up development. Education also makes people healthy through better health awareness. Education should be a continuing activity to enable the people to grow with the changing world.

The father of the Nation, Mahatma Gandhi, once said: "True democracy cannot be worked by twenty men sitting at the centre, it has to be worked from below by the people of every village." This goal of Indian democracy can be achieved by rural people only if they are involved in decision making and development. This in turn could depend upon the education and human resource development in rural areas.

Unless the large number of village people come forward with enthusiasm to participate in the development as partners of growth, the expected changes will not come in the rural sector and the people's planning will not achieve the desired results and growth. So, education should first change people so that they can change the villages. In this regard, the words of Jawaharlal Nehru will be worth remembering: "real change, comes, of course, from within the villages, from the people living in the village and is not imposed from outside." And the changes will come to the villages only if education moves into the mind of man with a purpose and an objective.

Education should, therefore, be a movement in society, so that it will drive away lawlessness, exploitation, insensitiveness and inhuman attitude, selfishness and disparities opening up the mind of the people for globalisation of knowledge and change. This will develop the rural genius to measure up to and face the challenges of development so much that there will be free flow of knowledge and expertise. It is said that the vast resources and hidden potential in rural region is the real wealth of India. Education should channelise this potential for development.

Panchayati raj institutions should invigorate and embolden people through a well-planned education to exercise their powers of democracy, without influence or interference from others. If people are not vigilant and alert, the benefits and funds, coming to them may go astray through covert actions of vested interests in society.

Rural people, slum dwellers and tribal people today face exploitation of various kinds. They are looked down upon sometimes treated as second class citizens in several places and facing threats and ill-treatment in society. They also fall victims of communalism. A majority of them are voiceless people. It is only through education that we can help them to join the mainstream of nation building. Education and panchayati raj brings technology to villages. Modern technology makes it possible to produce practically every consumer article by high standard in small scale sector in rural areas. Panchayati raj will be able to promote industries in rural and tribal areas.

Literacy mission in panchayati raj and continuing education of rural people will succeed only if there is proper awareness and awakening among the people. This will help the people to understand the link between education, panchayati raj and development. This understanding and awareness will give them a new spirit, new enthusiasm and motivation to respond positively to the call for participation in development.

In a nutshell, the functioning of panchayati raj can be made efficient, effective and result-oriented only if education plays an instrumental role in changing the attitude, thinking and outlook of the people. As a matter of policy, education should be a gateway to (1) Knowledge (2) Self-development and self-reliance (3) Employment (4) Better qualities and values of life and (5) Higher socio-economic status. Then only will the powers of democracy vested with the rural people give benefits of development to them.

The link between education, panchayat and development is well stated by Jawaharlal Nehru. To quote his words: "In every reorganised village, there must be three institutions—the village school, the village panchayat and village cooperatives." If these institutions move into the rural areas, it will lay a strong foundation of democracy in the village.

A social audit of our conscience on the eve of the 50th year of our Republic would reveal that we have to go miles and miles to achieve the socialistic goals of our democracy enshrined in the Constitution, Unless this is achieved, we cannot extend the facilities and benefits of democracy and development to the majority rural people living at the base of the Indian society. This goal can be achieved only through effective, efficient and result-oriented implementation of people's planning under every panchayat. We should also make education play a dominant role in opening up the mind of the rural people for globalisation of knowledge and to accelerate the pace of development.

In a nutshell, the nation's vision for the 21st century should be to give every Indian education, nutrious food, shelter, safe drinking water and other facilities of a decent, healthy and peaceful life. In other words, we should upgrade the socio-economic status of the majority people at the base of the Indian society to enable them to take off from the base and achieve more and more heights in living status. This is possible only if we implement the plans under the panchayati raj with a democratic and socialistic spirit and build up an educated and intelligent society.

9

Socialistic Pattern of Development

Socialistic pattern of development is the goal of our democracy. It helps us to achieve some kind of equality and justice in the matter of development. If the development moves upwards only forgetting the ground realities, that will lead to a lot of social and economic problems at the base of the society where the majority of the people live. So our efforts should be to make all the rights and privileges of democracy within the reach of each and every individual with equality and justice. There should be a uniform pattern of development everywhere.

The fact that India aims at a socialistic pattern of development is evident from the Preamble of the Constitution of Indian Republic, which, *inter alia*, pledged to secure for our people, justice social, economic and political; liberty of thought, expression, and belief, faith and worship, equality of status and opportunity and to promote among them all fraternity assuring the dignity of the individual and the unity of the nation. The crucial question today is why were we not able to give the full benefits of these rights to the people at the bottom of the society. It is time to think about it. In the new millennium, we should make a serious attempt to achieve the goal of a socialistic pattern of society where there will be peace and prosperity for all people.

In a democracy having its roots in socialism, education has to play a key role in enforcing a socialistic spirit in all its development programmes. This is essential to ensure equality and justice in development. This can be achieved only if education gives the best citizenship training to all persons. Education can help them to work with self-control and self-direction. Education can also inculcate in them a spirit of freedom, duty, responsibility and accountability in all their activities to achieve the true goal of democracy.

Indian democracy is embedded in socialism. The socialistic principles of equality, justice, liberty and fraternity are the pillars of our democracy. At the time of Independence, a majority of the people in the country were poor, living in backward areas. They were victims of poverty, misery and exploitation. There were also a lot of socio-economic contradictions. The national leaders were convinced that progress could be achieved only through socialistic principles. So, a socialistic pattern of society was a widely talked about topic in India immediately after Independence.

Obviously, to achieve the goal of socialistic pattern of development, we have to secure all the rights and privileges enshrined in the Constitution for all the people.

But look at the plight of the people. See whether the people who go to bed at night with an empty stomach are in thousands or in millions. Look at the plight of millions of working children and voiceless people who are victims of large-scale exploitation. Then we will be able to understand that with the so-called population explosion, the problems of the poor people, the downtrodden, the working people and the voiceless people have increased making their life a struggle between man against man and man against circumstances. The main reason for this situation may be attributed to population growth. But, surprisingly, population explosion has not affected the life of the people in the higher strata of the society. There are other reasons for the worsening of living conditions of the poor and these can be identified as slow growth in rural and backward areas, no growth in tribal areas, uneven development and absence of dynamic action in the lower strata of the society. Thus a lot of socio-economic inequalities and contradictions are still prevalent in our society. Viewed in this light, perhaps, we are far away from the goal of a socialistic pattern of society.

Jawaharlal Nehru, the first Prime Minister of India, was convinced that socialism alone could solve the problems of the Indian people. Nehru, therefore, set a definite goal to achieve a socialistic pattern of development and spoke eloquently hundreds of thousands of words in and outside parliament to promote this ideal. Nehru's words and deeds to promote a socialistic pattern of society are the bedrock in the history of free India. But, subsequently, it lost its momentum and, in course of time, lost its direction. As a result, today our economic system is more or less a mountain with a small percentage of population in the upper areas and a large number of people living in he downward areas branded as middle class, lower middle class, poor, under-privileged, downtrodden and so on. Needless to say, their social uplift, economic progress and prosperity are possible only through socialistic pattern of development. A look at the socialistic principles of our democracy as enshrined in our Constitution clearly points to a socialistic pattern of development. But how far have we moved towards this goal. Let us go to remote rural areas, tribal areas and slums of India and knock at the doors of the people there, and we will be convinced that we are nowhere near a socialistic pattern of society. And when we see that about half of the population of metropolitan cities like Mumbai are living in slums or similar conditions that will give us an idea about the socio-economic contradictions in our society. This is not to make the tremendous progress and achievements made by us after independence insignificant but to point out that contradictions and disparities still exist in a big way in our society.

In this context, the observation of Dr. B. R. Ambedkar is an eye-opener to us and still relevant to our socio-economic conditions. While presenting the draft Constitution in the Constituent Assembly, he *inter alia*, said: "On 26th January, we are going to enter a life of contradictions. In politics, we will have equality and in social and economic life, we will have inequality. In politics, we will be recognising the principle of 'one man one vote' and 'one vote one value'. In our social and economic life, we will by reasons of our social and economic structure continue to deny one man, one value." And he then asked—how long shall we deny equality in our social, and economic life?

That even after 50 years of Independence and epoch-making progress and achievements in all sectors, the majority people continue to live a life of socio-economic contradictions, inequality and injustice is no secret. Now, it is clear that if we want to give democratic rights, privileges and values and the benefits of development to the poor people, working people, downtrodden, village people, tribal people and other underprivileged and voiceless people, who form the basic structure of our society, we have to minimise the inequalities and contradictions and move towards a socialistic pattern of society. How long it will take to accomplish this task is a crucial question before us. But, come what may, this should be our vision for the 21st century, only then can we enter the new millennium, with the entire people with us. We should instil confidence among the poor and voiceless people, dynamise and activise them through decentralised planning so that the basic structure of the society will be a strong foundation for our future progress.

Paradoxically, removing the life of contradictions from the Indian society is not a bed of roses. It is a herculean task. There are obstacles to be removed. There are hurdles to be crossed. There are old socio-economic structures to be reformed. When we do these exercises, care has to be taken to ensure that the existing upper strata of the society and the progress already achieved are not disturbed. Anyhow, to keep the spirit of our Constitution and our democratic traditions, and to help the majority people at the bottom of the society to join the mainstream of national development, we should achieve the goal of socialistic pattern of development. To achieve success in this direction, the government, the people and the non-governmental organisations should come together and work together as partners of change and growth.

Our future goal should, therefore, be to remove the social and economic contradictions, paving the way for a socialistic pattern of development and help the poor and downtrodden people in the lower strata to join the mainstream of national development. There should be equality of opportunity in the matter of education with special support to the weak in employment and other economic activities, so that we can undo disparities widely prevalent in our society.

Equality of opportunity in education is very important to achieve the goal of socialistic pattern of development. In this light, the observation of Kothari Commission is a guiding spirit to us when we step into the next millennium:

> One of the important social objectives of education is to equalise opportunity enabling the backward or under-privileged classes and individuals to use education as a lever for the improvement of their condition. Every society that values social justice and is anxious to improve the lot of the common man and cultivate all available talent must ensure progressive equality of opportunity to all sections of population. This is the only guarantee for the building up of an egalitarian and human society in which exploitation of the weak will be minimised.

Our efforts to move towards a socialistic pattern of society will succeed only if there is an educational system on the above lines. The principles of such an education should not only be knowledge-giving and skill-making but also giving citizenship training and developing the full potential of the individual. Unless we achieve equality of opportunity in education making the entire spectrum of education within the reach of all people, high or low, we will not be able to establish equality of opportunity in the socio-economic sector. There is an imperative need for a change of thinking, change of attitude and outlook and change of consciousness on the part of all to get clearcut results in this direction. If we do not take dynamic action, the clarion call for equality and justice in the socio-economic sector will go astray and the dream of the majority people for a progressive life will remain unrealised. As such, education is the primary and powerful factor to lay a strong foundation for a socialistic pattern of society.

The second and equally important factor is the panchayat raj system, which is the key for grassroots level planning to dynamise the basic structure of the society where the majority people live below the normal standards. Decentralisation of planning through panchayat raj will help them to actively participate in nation building and become partners of growth. The aids and assistance that we give to the people at the grassroots level to solve their problems of living temporarily, cannot be considered as a solid foundation for a permanent socio-economic uplift paving the way for higher socio-economic status. Although it provides solace and comfort to their immediate problems, it will not help them to climb up the ladder of opportunity in education and employment with enlarged scope for best citizenship training and vocational guidance. Only through long-term plans can we minimise inequalities and contradictions in the socio-economic front, clearing the way for permanent and total uplift of the people living at the basic structure of our society. This will, no doubt, help the majority people in the third world within India to benefit by democracy and development and move upwards in the socio-economic ladder.

Needless to say, Mahatma Gandhi had provided enough inspiration to establish a secular, socialistic and democratic society. For instance, consider the thoughts of Gandhiji: "I shall work for an India in which the poorest shall feel that it is their country in whose making they have an effective voice, an India where there shall be no high class and low class of people, an India in which all communities shall live in perfect harmony. This is the India of my dreams." Obviously,

Gandhiji's dream was for equality and justice and a socialistic society where the welfare of the individual will be the responsibility of all.

So, our vision for the 21st century will be a socialistic pattern of society where the majority people at the base of the Indian social and economic structure will have equal opportunities in educational, social and economic activities. That will be a society with minimum inequalities and injustice in line with our requirement. A multi-religious society has to be secular in character, social in conduct and democratic in function and then only will there be freedom, peace, tolerance and cooperation among all sections of the population, which are indispensable to achieve total development with balanced growth and benefit to all.

It is high time that we put our democracy on the socialistic rail in its proper prospective. Proper and amicable solution to the million problems of the people can be found only through (1) full and honest decentralisation of power at the village level, (2) equality of opportunity in educational, social and economic activities, and (3) a policy of 'education for all and employment for all' helping the entire people to join the mainstream of national progress. Let us all be partners of growth and share the benefits in the new millennium.

At this juncture, let us remember the words of Jawaharlal Nehru. On one occasion, speaking in the Lok Sabha, Nehru said, "We talk about a socialistic pattern of society, industrialisation, of higher standards and so on. What is really necessary is to activise and dynamise the base of the Indian social structure. I want the House to appreciate this phrase. No doubt there must be approaches from the top but there has been too much activising from the top layers of the society all the time. We do not solve our problems unless we activise the base of the Indian society, which means millions and millions of villagers, millions of workers and small earners, unemployed people and people on the land. They are the base of the Indian society."

The benefits of development and democratic rights and values should move downwards to activise the base of Indian society. It should move down through decentralised channels. This will reduce inequalities and minimise contradictions and ensure equality and justice in the lower strata of the society.

10

Alcohol-Drug-Tobacco Tragedy in Society

Alcohol-drug-tobacco addiction is becoming an inseperable lifestyle of man, particularly in developing countries. It is not only a health problem but also a social problem in the poor families. It has been reported that a high percentage of hospital beds are occupied by patients with alcohol-drug-tobacco-related illnesses. The cost of treatment is also exorbitantly high. Thousands of people are falling victims to road accidents caused by drinking and driving. Three out of ten accidents at work are caused by alcohol. The habit motivates people to commit crimes and also suicides. The majority of the crimes like violence, rapes, assaults, thefts, hooliganism, murders, etc., are related to this habit. There is degeneration of values as a result of this habit. The diseases caused by alcohol, drugs and tobacco affects all important organs of man. In the younger generation, studies have brought to light that increased alcohol habit leads to malformation of important nerve system in vital organs. The fact that a reasonable number of young people fall victims of the habit every year is a matter of shock to parents and concern to community. Such habits spoil not only the future of the children but also adversely affect the family, and the nation at large. So, we should come up with a long-term policy to check the habit among the adults and also to keep away the younger generation from the habit.

The fact that a large number of young people are falling victims of the alcohol-drug-tobacco habit is of course a matter of serious concern to any nation, as it is upon them the future of the nation depends. Continuous alcohol-drug-tobacco habit erodes their health, character and quality of mind and thereby the wealth of the nation.

In recent years, there has been an alarming increase in alcohol consumption, drug addiction and tobacco use in our society. This growing habit, particularly among the youth and working population, is becoming more and more pronounced year after year. It erodes the health of the people, and therefore, the wealth of the nation. The socio-economic problems and challenges arising out of it are formidable. It drains a lot of energy and slows down the development.

Alcohol, drug and tobacco are fast becoming a degenerating force in our society, particularly so when it is combined with violence. Violence is widely prevalent and alcohol, they say, is directly or indirectly supporting it by motivating the individual to resort to violent activities. As a result, the alcohol-related health problems cause a severe strain on the life of the individual and the social fabric of the family and the community at large. Alcohol, when it is combined with tobacco and drug, as a trio, becomes a force to reckon with to achieve narrow goals. And the weaker sections, the unemployed youth, the students and other vulnerable groups are, knowingly or unknowingly, falling victims to alcohol-combined violence resulting in a serious setback not only to their own health but also to that of their family.

According to the World Health Organisation, the problems relating to alcohol rank among the major health problems of the world. Some years ago, an official of the World Health Organisation corroborated that the alcohol-related problems even constitute an important obstacle for development and threaten to overwhelm health services unless appropriate measures are taken at the right time. Research studies have revealed that a high proportion of the hospital beds are occupied, year after year, by physically and mentally derailed victims of alcohol and violence. To these should be added the large number of people who fall victims of accidents caused by drinking and driving.

Research studies have brought to light that alcohol consumption and the consequent violence coupled with rash and negligence driving cause a third and a half of all road deaths. The drinking habit causes three out of ten accidents at work and results in loss of production. In many cities and rural areas, it is the main cause of crime, which is alarmingly increasing day by day.

Uncontrolled drinking habit among the bread earners of the family promotes quarrel and poverty in the family. Wife and child beating are common scenes in rural areas and slums. The mental health of the individual goes down in alcoholic drain and lifelong emotional scars are left on spouses and children. The growing habit of drinking takes away in full or a good part of the income of the individual. Thus he is unable to provide the needed support to give essential food and other necessities of life to the family members. The children of some alcoholic parents are often in a pitiable life situation. The children caught in between quarrels of parents and social conflicts, lose all interest in life. They also lose proper guidance and direction. Unbearable of such torturing situation, children in such families run away from home, falling victims to child labour or delinquency. Thus the children of parents who are habitual drinkers are living under a number of risks. They risk being beaten, neglected or undernourished. But beyond that they may risk long-term harm from memory of terrible or even tragic scenes. In a nutshell, the individual as well as the family members suffer serious psychological and physical problems affecting their health and life.

Largescale flow of poor quality alcohol into the slums and rural areas make the life of the people not only miserable and horrible but also easily susceptible to all sorts of diseases. Thus alcohol today is a rising tide eroding the heath of the individual and the family, and consequently that of the society. Apart from the risk of being attacked by diseases affecting the heart, liver, lungs and other vital organs of the body, the children and youth in their family sometimes face discrimination by other people. They suffer development of their personality, family, professional and civic attitude and qualities of life. They are often misled and driven into anti-social and violent activities. In the absence of proper guidance at home, they grow in an unfavourable living environment and develop negative attitude and violent behaviour, as being widely witnessed now. Thus the French slogan "Where parents drink, it is children who pay" is most relevant and true in our society.

The children and youth who are forced into the habit of drinking and drug addiction are long-term sufferers. Research has revealed that drinking habit among the children and younger people below a certain age cripples their future health, as it affects the formation and growth of the vital nervous system in the body. That a good percentage of youth in our country are acquiring this habit for one reason or another is a matter of serious concern to the nation.

Today we are living in an environment where violence and crimes are increasing alarmingly; crime against girls and women, weaker sections; murders like father killing wife or son, wife killing husband, son killing mother or father, brother killing brother, and so on and so forth. We are also frequently hearing about wife and children committing suicide due to unbearable living conditions at home. All these violent activities can be linked to alcohol, which is overtly or covertly, playing a role in promoting these crimes and anti-social activities.

The number of girls and women acquiring the habit of drinking is also increasing. In women, alcohol brings about serious psychological and social consequences, particularly so when they are in the child-bearing age. Alcohol affects not only the health of the mother but also that of the child.

Thus it can be seen that the alcohol—a mood-changing habit—is slowly and steadily becoming a health destroyer among the people. When they fall a victim to the alcohol dependence syndrome, the alcohol takes control of their health and life. In our society, the alcohol-combined violent behaviour promotes death on the roads—in thousands—and ruins one's own earning capacity, lower the socio-economic status of the individual, motivates the individual to neglect wife and children, and acts as a stimulator of quarrels, murders, rapes, assaults, thefts, burglary, hooliganism and so on. All these activities erode the health and degenerate the moral, social and other values of life and often destroy the family culture itself.

The first aim of the World Health Organisation's alcohol programme is to alert the world to the devastating spread of alcohol-related health problems. The World Health Assembly on more than one occasion recognised that the problems relating to alcohol, particularly the excessive consumption, as one of the world's major public health challenges.

No nation may be willing to lose the health and power of the people, particularly the youth. Several nations have already come forward with concrete plans to fight the alcohol menace and save time, health and energy of the youth. The World Health Organisation has set clearcut guidelines for the purpose.

There is an imperative need to provide education on alcohol-related problems from the school stage itself. There should also be brain storming sessions meant for youth and other vulnerable sections. This should also be included in the National Literacy Mission Programme. The role of the media, particularly TV, films, radio and newspapers are very important in this direction. Panchayati raj institutions, social clubs, voluntary organisations, educational institutions, hospitals and even educated individuals can play a positive role in preventing abuse of alcohol and saving the health of the people. There should also be intensive counselling and treatment programmes to the victims of alcohol-dependence syndrome. Legislative measures prohibiting sale of alcohol to younger people, restricting the timings of sale of alcohol, introduction of prohibition, discouraging establishing brewing/ distillery industries, etc., are measures that will help in achieving positive results.

The problems caused by the increasing alcohol habit can be solved only with active community participation.

Tobacco is another threat to man's progress. It is a serious health hazard. But still the habit is on the increase in developing nations. It is considered as a high ranking public enemy in developed countries. While rigid controls are being exercised in these countries to cut down the habit, the manufacturers are concentrating on developing countries for their market. It has been found that tobacco use in one from or another is on the increase in rural areas and among younger people. The cost of treating tobacco-related ills is said to be two and a half times more than the profit from the tobacco industry. Cigarette is known to contain about 4,000 chemicals and 200 poisonous elements. This shows how dangerous it is for health.

According to WHO, every year tobacco causes 3.5 million deaths globally. This means 10,000 deaths every day. By the year 2020, experts say, tobacco will kill 10 million of the current 1.1 billion smokers in the world. Nearly seven million tobacco related deaths would occur in developing countries. That tobacco consumption has increased considerably among children, youth and women is a matter of concern to all.

India being the third largest producer in the world produces 5,76,200 metric tons of tobacco. An estimated 0.4 million people are engaged in tobacco work. A total of 100 billion cigarettes and 850 million beedies are manufactured in India annually. Tobacco is also widely used in smokeless/ chewing form.

Annually about 6,35,000 deaths are attributed to tobacco. India has one of the world's highest incidence of oral cancer. Other avoidable tobacco-related diseases are cancer of the respiratory tract, coronary heart disease, chronic obstructive lung disease, still-births, low birth-weight infants, etc. In India about half of all cancers in women are attributed to tobacco use.

Environmental tobacco smoke is highly injurious to health. Children grow up surrounded by smoke at home and outside. It causes serious health problems in them. The WHO believes that every child has the right to grow up without tobacco. Our goal should be a tobacco-free social behaviour at every home.

Unfortunately, the public health crisis caused by tobacco is worsening in developing countries particularly among children above 10 and weaker sections of the society.

Children continuously exposed to environmental tobacco smoke get more cough and colds, respiratory infections, bronchitis, asthma, impaired lung function, middle-ear infection, eye and nasal irritation, etc.

Thus it can be seen that while alcohol and tobacco are useful to the people who work in this field, it is a serious health hazard to millions of people. In addition to huge hospital expenditure, there are innumerable socio-economic problems. The nation is also losing a lot of energy and talent on account of this.

It is high time that we take suitable measures to tackle the health and socio-economic problems involved. The following aspects are important in this direction.

1. Health education at all levels involving medical professional, educated citizens, trade union, student groups, parents and other associations to keep people away from tobacco-alcohol-drug habit, particularly children, youth and poor sections. Health education should be introduced as a subject in all educational institutions.
2. Ban advertisements of tobacco products.
3. Legislation to prohibit use of drugs, tobacco and alcohol in public places.
4. Legislation to ban sale of tobacco, drugs and alcohol to people below 18 years of age.

5. Use of fiscal policies to discourage use of tobacco and alcohol.
6. Alternate industry, trade and employment to replace tobacco-drugs and alcohol-related trade.
7. Creating smoke-free homes.
8. Strict control on the quality of alcohol, preventing use of cheap and low quality of alcohol by poor people, time limit for sale of alcohol-related products, etc., will also help to reduce the health problems caused by it.
9. Controlled quantity and quality of alcohol consumption among adults should be monitored.

In the new century, there is need for a new effort aimed at to reducing and minimising the health and socio-economic problems of drug, tobacco and alcohol.

11

Changing Health—Challenges to Survival

We have been witnessing tremendous and marvellous progress in the field of medicine. With new discoveries coming to light every day, the health scenario is changing rapidly. But, simultaneously, the challenges of survival are also increasing. In spite of all our achievements, a number of new generation diseases headed by the mysterious AIDS are haunting man. Most of the advanced medical facilities are available to the people in the upper layer of the society living in urban areas. The majority of the population of the developing world living in rural areas are not getting these facilities and benefits. There is inequality and injustice. Even today, a major portion of the health expenditure is in favour of the urban people. The advanced facilities are not within the reach of the majority of the poor and rural people. So, there should be a major shift in the priorities of the health sector, from urban to rural and from developed to undeveloped areas of the world. The worsening environmental degradation and the poor living conditions of the majority people, make the earth a breeding ground for all virus. Health education, prevention of diseases, timely immunisation, advanced treatment facilities for the rural people, clean environment and drinking water, change of lifestyle in favour of good health, etc., should be our future priorities to achieve the goal of health for all. And our slogan of Health for All should continue till the full health status is achieved by the rural people.

The golden maxim 'Health is wealth' has great relevance today. Most people in the developing world are today poor and have no wealth because they are not healthy. But the fact remains that without wealth, they cannot be healthy as the advanced health and medical facilities are not within their reach. For any developing nation, each drop of human energy lost is a real loss and the huge amount of energy being lost every day due to ill-health of the people erodes the wealth of the nation.

During the 20th century there has been spectacular achievements in the field of health and medical technology. As a result, the world is today moving fast towards a healthier society. These achievements have helped to increase the average life expectancy to 66 years, due to control of several communicable diseases, reduction mortality rate and prevention of killer-diseases through immunisation. Hopefully mankind can look forward for better health facilities in the new century.

But, paradoxically, there is grave inequality and injustice in providing health benefits to the majority rural population living in the lower strata of the society in the developing and least developed countries. That we spent a lion's share of the health budget on hospitals and urban population is no secret. At least a half of the global population have no access to latest health and medical facilities either because of the exorbitant cost or distance. Sometimes, they have to go miles to get health care facilities. They are far away from the global health goal which envisages "Every individual should enjoy his or her full health potential throughout the lifespan and be socially, economically and mentally productive and able to have a better quality of life."

Modern medical facilities, health care and preventive methods are indispensable to achieve the above goal. But for the majority of the people of the third world countries the goal cannot be realised in the distant future. Modern health facilities and preventive methods are not within the reach of these people, mainly because of poor income, illiteracy and non-availability of medical health facilities. The health condition of these people can be improved only if we take the modern health facilities at affordable cost to them. A change of attitude and outlook is therefore indispensable to achieve this goal in the near future. In this light, the following observation in the *World Health Report 1998* is worth reading:

> Both the absolute poor and the non-poor are trapped in a situation where economic growth and social development are interdependent. Low incomes mean limited capacity to save and invest, limited means for obtaining health services, high risk of personal illness, limitations on mobility and limited access to education, information and training. Poor parents cannot provide their children with opportunities for better health and education to improve their lot. Lack of motivation, hope and incentives, creates a barrier to growth and poverty is passed from one generation to the next.

Today we number 6 billion, paradoxically, a majority of them live in developing countries. About 80 per cent of the population in developing countries are living in a very bad condition, and according to reports about 1000 million people are absolutely poor. Many millions of people in developing countries endure a precarious existence in shanty towns, slums, refugee camps and squatter settlements. Their living environment is far away from being a healthy one. The non-availability of safe water and absence of sanitational and drainage facilities encourages a host of diseases—typhoid, cholera, hepatitis, poliomyelitis, dysentery, amoebiasis, etc.

The fuels burned in the earth by about half of the world's population as the major source of domestic energy result in between 400 and 500 million people suffering from serious indoor air pollution.

Scarcity of food, overcrowding, perpetual stress, alienation—all these aspects create fertile conditions for severe mental health problems.

The urban poor are caught between the evils of industrialisation and backwardness, and added to their already crippling burden of infectious diseases and malnutrition is a set of new non-communicable diseases commonly associated with hasty industrialisation and the indiscriminate use of chemicals.

For the overwhelming majority of the poor people, shelter, safe water, facilities for removal of household and human wastes, health care and educational services and such other facilities of life still remain a distant goal. Generation upon generation is living in most deplorable conditions in slums and settlements.

Malnutrition, the eternal sign of poverty, is one of the persistent health problems of the urban poor. According to WHO, "the energy protein in some 145 million children under five years old are insufficient." Not merely the shortage of food is to blame but much more complex problems, including "inadequate preparation and storage of food, lack of knowledge about nutritional needs in infancy and in childhood and the effects of repeated infectious diseases" are also to be blamed. In addition, the breakdown of the traditional extended family in urban settlements directly affects the quality of care. According to reports, millions of children are living in unsafe places and streets in different countries of the world. Living environment for these children is extremely bad.

Water, as we know, is life. We can't live without safe water. It is also a major medium for disease transmission including typhoid and cholera. In the third world countries, five million children die every year from diarrhoeal diseases. The major villain of this global tragedy is unsafe water. The sheer scale of waterborn diseases is truly staggering. Poliomyelitis, guinea-worm infection, malaria, yellow fever, dengue fever, river blindness, schistosomiasis—these are just a handful of the more commonly known ones. The bad news is that throughout the tropics, matters are getting worse, not better. Malaria and other vector-borne diseases previously confined to the rural areas, have now found ideal breeding ground in the slums. Emergence of urban malaria is yet another disturbing factor. In brief it can be said that the majority of the population in developing countries is exposed to various diseases, poverty and environmental pollution.

Thus, providing modern health facilities to the majority poor people in the world is indeed a challenge at the dawn of the new century. We should meet this challenge with a commitment so that we can achieve encouraging results in the area of rural health. The destruction or survival of the people would depend upon our commitment and dedication to provide better health and higher socio-economic status to the rural and poor people.

Another important challenge in the new age will be the increasing death of people particularly children and those in the productive age group. According to WHO three out of four people in the least developed countries today are dying before the age of 50. This year it is 21 million deaths—two out of five worldwide will be under 50's including 10 million children. Over seven million will be men and women in most productive years of their life. Reducing these premature deaths is one of the greatest challenges facing humanity at the dawn of the 21st century.

In spite of the marvellous advances in the field of health and medicine, a series of dangerous diseases headed by AIDS are haunting humanity. The important among these diseases are cardiovascular diseases and stroke, cancer, tuberculosis, deficiency diseases, alcohol-drug-tobacco caused diseases, pregnancy-related diseases and environmental pollution-caused diseases. That these diseases are increasing year after year is a matter of serious concern to the entire world. Unless drastic measures are taken to prevent and control these diseases, there will be disastrous consequences and a socio-economic crisis in the world.

The root causes of these diseases are poverty, malnutrition, non-availability of safe drinking water, changing lifestyles associated with alcohol, tobacco and drugs, illiteracy, indisciplined life, discrimination, inadequate health care, environmental pollution and rapid urbanisation. So the major effort should be to remove these root causes and improve the socio-economic conditions and quality of life of the majority people in the third world. This will help to reduce the burden of the health and medical services and to effectively control the diseases. Prevention of diseases will also save a lot of money to the family and government.

Of all the diseases, AIDS is becoming more and more curious to the whole world. Its alarming increase in developing and least developed countries questions even the future survival of people. According to WHO in 1998 over six million people including half-a-million children were infected with AIDS. At the dawn of the new century, 40 million people worldwide are likely to be infected. This is far beyond the expectations of the past. In the cases of TB, three million deaths are occurring every year and an estimated eight million new cases emerge in a year. It is a paradox that most of these cases emerge mostly in poor and developing countries. While cancer claims six million lives a year, cardiovascular diseases and stroke take a toll of 12 million. The alcohol-tobacco diseases are also on the increase. In addition, a large number of women and children in rural areas and slums are victims of deficiency diseases like protein energy deficiency, iodine deficiency, vitamin A and B 12 deficiency, iron and fluride deficiency and so on. WHO indicates that about 265 million children in 75 countries are victims of vitamin A deficiency, the most prevalent cause of blindness. Similarly, most women and children in poor countries are victims of anaemia.

We have to recognise the fact that the tremendous progress of medicine achieved and available in India has helped to improve the overall health status. But we cannot ignore the fact that these medical advances are mainly confined to urban areas and its beneficiaries are mainly people in the upper layer of the society. It has not moved into the rural areas to the needed extent to give the same benefits to the people in the lower strata of the society. In other words, it has not been able to respond adequately to the needs of the rural people. Advanced medical services and drugs are so costly that the majority of the poor villagers cannot afford it. It is not within their reach either because of the cost factor or because of the distance.

The Alma Ata Conference on Primary Health Care organised by WHO/UNICEF in 1978 defined the Primary Health Care as an "essential health care based on specifically sound and socially acceptable methods and technology accessible to individuals and families in their country through their full participation and at a cost the community and the country can afford to maintain at every stage of their development in the spirit of self-reliance and self-determination."

In order to prevent most of the preventable diseases and provide effective treatment for control of diseases, there should be combined efforts in rural areas. The objectives of such a health programme will aim at improvement of living conditions, health education and prevention, and treatment and rehabilitation. As already mentioned, the advanced medical facilities available for people in the urban sector of the society are not within the reach of the common man in rural areas. For most of the village people health and medical services are confined of Primary Health Care Centres and at best Taluk Hospitals. Moreover, unsafe drinking water, absence of sanitation, bad living conditions and illiteracy make rural areas a fertile ground for 80 per cent of the common diseases. Thus, whether it is mentally ill, victims of malnutrition, handicapped persons, working children or victims of various preventable and communicable diseases, many of them are in villages and slums. Through the erosion of health of these people, the nation is losing a lot of energy.

Health is not merely the absence of disease but a state of physical, mental and social well-being. It is the health that helps the individual to develop his full potential and utilise it for sustainable development in rural areas. Due to the wide gap between the health needs of the rural people and the facilities available, their health status is far below the requirements. Although their health is in the priority sector now, the infrastructure available is not sufficient to the vast requirement of rural areas.

During the last 50 years, a lion's share of the health expenditure, both in the public and the private sector has been either in or around the urban areas, i.e., cities and towns having a population of more than a lakh, which consists of only about 20 per cent of the nation's population. An inadequate percentage of health expenditure is only going to our rural people. Sometime, even the Primary Health Care Centres are located in far away places. There is, therefore, an imperative need to shift the emphasis of health policy to rural areas and spend 75 per cent of the expenditure in rural areas till some kind of equality and justice is achieved.

Health of Rural Children

It is said that today's children are tomorrow's nation builders. At least 30 per cent of the rural people is below the age of 20. Most of the rural children are victims of malnutrition and various diseases, Above all, most of them are living in poor families. If the present conditions continue to prevail, they will not be able to grow healthy. Article 39 of the directive principles of the Constitution of India stipulates that children are given opportunities and facilities to develop in a healthy manner, and in conditions of freedom and dignity and that childhood and youth are protected against exploitation and against moral and material abandonment. In spite of the health promotion activities and corrective actions taken, the living conditions and educational progress of children in rural areas are low. Therefore, there is need to have a fresh look at the state of affairs in rural areas keeping in view the importance of rural children and youth in nation building.

The government of India's policy for children assures constitutional fulfilment and adequate services before and after birth, through the period of growth and to ensure full mental, physical and social development. This focus on development of human resources among the children and youth are yet to enter remote rural areas in a big way. There is alarming increases in diseases, malnutrition, child labour, illiteracy and unhealthy living conditions. Of the 320 million children below 20 years of age, the majority is in villages. So also is the case of youth. So, we should give top priority to rural health so that the quality of life of the people and their health can be improved in line with the national requirement.

MAGNITUDE OF THE RURAL HEALTH PROBLEMS

The health problems of the rural people are linked to their socio-economic problems. If their socio-economic status are improved, most of the diseases affecting the rural people can be prevented and the related health problems solved. On an estimate, about 350 million people are below the poverty line and a good number is just on the poverty line or a little above. This category of people are facing a lot of socio-economic problems, which force them to live in the lower strata of the society. The serious problems affecting their life are illiteracy, unemployment and poor income, non-availability of essential food items, and malnutrition, non-availability of safe drinking water and lack of sanitational facilities. If all these socio-economic problems of the rural people are solved, it will help to prevent a vast number of diseases and solve their health problems. The best health and medical services should be made available to these people. So, our first task would be to bring about some kind of equality and justice in the matter of rural people. Top priority has to be given to rural health and allied problems till they become equal to the people in the upper strata of the society.

For the last 50 years, we have witnessed a tremendous development in the socio-economic and health sectors. But the beneficiaries of this advance were limited. The per capita health expenditure of a rural citizen is far below when compared to that of the urban citizen. It is, therefore, necessary that we should bridge the gap first and then maintain per capita health expenditure on an somewhat equitable basis in respect of rural people and urban people. This is possible only if the health sector is linked to socio-economic problems such as poverty, malnutrition, unemployment, unsafe drinking water, illiteracy and non-availability of sanitational facilities, shortage of shelter and crowded living environment. In a nutshell, serious efforts should be made to remove the basic causes of the diseases and health problems of the rural people. This way only, can we find a permanent solution to the health problems of the rural people. In this direction, the following aspects are important.

Malnutrition

It is a well known fact that many people in rural areas and slums are victims of malnutrition. This is particularly true of women and children. The causes of malnutrition may be identified as poverty, shortage of essential food items, low income, etc. It has been reported that at least a hundred million children in rural areas are living below poverty line and an equal number is only marginally better. The infant mortality in the low income group is very high.

The important categories of nutritional problems are given as under:

a) Protein-energy Malnutrition (PEM) especially in children and pregnant women.

b) Obesity and consequent increase in non-communicable diseases among the affluent sections.

c) Micro-nutrient deficiency of iron, iodine and vitamin A, and associated health problems.

In order to prevent all preventable diseases, the problem of malnutrition should be solved. It calls for nationwide efforts in view of the magnitude the problem and the large number of people involved. To achieve the goal, there are only two ways. The first one is to make available all essential food items to the rural people at subsidised prices or/free of cost. The second choice is to improve the overall economic status of the rural family permanently by providing them gainful employment and enhancing their purchasing power.

Safe Drinking Water

According to estimates, a large number of people in the rural areas do not have access to safe water. Paradoxically 80 per cent of the diseases affecting rural population is waterborne, Unless, we provide clean and safe water to all villages, it will not be possible to fully control and eliminate most of these preventable diseases.

The common diseases continue to dominate the rural areas in spite of the rigid measures taken by the government. Hence safe water projects should be linked to rural health programme. This is necessary to find a permanent solution to the rural health problems.

Crowded Homes and Living Environment

Overcrowded homes in villages and slums are potential sources of diseases. As most of these families have a number of children and other members, the bread-earners with their meagre income are unable to provide sufficient quantity food and a clean living environment. Thus the poor income, unlimited number of children and extended families, poverty, and illiteracy deteriorate the living conditions in rural areas. Increased income through gainful employment, education, limited family, shelter and clean surroundings will help a lot to improve the overall living conditions and remove one of the root causes of increasing diseases in villages. Sanitary facilities, waste disposal systems, roads and drinking water facilities will help the villages to keep away these diseases. So the 'small family and clean environment' campaign should be part of the rural health programmes. In the absence of such an action, the more we cure the diseases, the more will be the new cases. Thus, there will be an unending incidence of diseases in rural areas.

Stigma and Prejudices

In our country, even in educated regions and states, social stigma attached to various diseases like TB, leprosy, AIDS, etc., are still a cause for the spread of the diseases. It appears that while there is no stigma or prejuidice against some highly contagious diseases, there is deep-rooted stigma, prejudice and anxiety about diseases which are less or not dangerous at all. We will be able to change this situation by health education at all levels. If people are properly educated about the real nature and scientific facts of the disease, that will help to clear the mind and the way to identify and treat all cases in the early stage itself, preventing its spread.

Health Care Centres and Hospitals

In many remote villages and tribal areas, health centres and hospitals are located in far away places and therefore not easily accessible to the people. In a number of villages lack of roads and transport keep them away from prompt and regular health service. In a number of health centres and hospitals, shortage of staff, medicines and space and latest equipments is indeed a problem. Moreover, the service of highly qualified experts is not within the reach of the poor rural and tribal people. It is therefore necessary that we should have full-fledged hospitals and health centres for them. Even today about 15 per cent of the population does not have access to health services in poor countries.

Community Action

Prevention of diseases and promotion of health is the duty of every citizen. Several root causes of ill-health and diseases in rural areas can be fully removed only with the active involvement of the community. Health problems of the rural people are so complicated that nothing tangible can be achieved without the involvement of the people. Another important channel for rural health is non-governmental organisations.

In addition to this, the individuals can, individually and collectively, strengthen the community involvement with the health sector. Apart from mobilising resources, manpower, money and materials, they can strengthen the community systems, educational channels, creation of clean living environment and help monitoring health programmes. This will no doubt help to speed-up up the implementation of health programmes.

Illiteracy and Health Education

The main hurdle to progress and healthy life in rural areas is illiteracy. It is estimated that about 65 per cent of the rural population is illiterate. Thus illiteracy and lack of education is the important bottleneck in finding a permanent solution to the health problems of the rural people. At present a majority of the rural population is not covered by regular education or the multimedia communication. Hence, health education should be an integral part of the rural health programme. It should be introduced in all educational institutions and also in the adult literacy programme.

Health of the rural people is indeed a political, social and economic issue. There is need to strengthen a communication link within the rural homes and outside. Health education is a primary factor to achieve good results in rural health sector. Literacy forms the basis for the education of the rural people, who are mostly illiterates. The rural people should have the right to information and knowledge, right to participation, right to demand facility for treatment, and equality and justice in health matters. Education is the gateway to these rights and privileges. Health education also helps to remove social stigmas and prejudices from the minds of the people.

Today the main and affordable means of information to the rural people is newspapers, but it is not withing their reach. It is said that 93 per cent of the newspaper readership is in urban and semi-urban areas. The main cause for this state of affairs is illiteracy. So unless we remove illiteracy and improve the educational status of the rural people, it is difficult to bring them within the reach of the growing information world. Similarly, in the case of radio, 80 per cent of the sets are in urban areas. At present, it has been reported that only about six million radio sets are available to about 525 million rural people. In regard to TV coverage also, the position is not encouraging. Although 86.5 per cent of the population is covered by TV, most of the TV sets are in urban and semi-urban areas. For the majority rural population, only about 60,000 TV sets are available in community centres. In the case of films too, most of the theatres are in urban areas. Thus almost all the means of modern communication are not within the easy reach of the rural people, the poor people, the illiterate people and the downtrodden. The information gap between the rural people and the urban people is very wide. There is an imperative need to improve the communication link with the rural people as media education is very vital for better health and improved quality of life. Serious efforts should be made to integrate this with health promotion activities in rural areas.

National Policy

National programmes to combat major public health problems are being implemented in the country. Although progress has been achieved in this direction, the disease burden in rural areas continue to increase alarmingly due to unhealthy conditions prevailing there.

The Ninth Plan documents indicate that there will be absolute and total commitment to:

1) Improve facilities for health care and enhance quality of primary health care in urban and rural areas through an optimally functioning primary health care system.
2) Appropriate strengthening of the secondary and tertiary care institutions,
3) Improve efficiency and build up effective referral linkages, between the existing, primary, secondary and tertiary care institutions.
4) Develop human resources for health, adequate in quantity and appropriate in quality, programme and people-orientation.
5) Effectively implement the provision of food and drug safety.
6) Enhance research capabilities and strengthening basic, clinical and health system research.

The plan perspectives are very encouraging and result-oriented. But, as much as rural areas are concerned, there is a need for special emphasis in view of the majority population involved and the increasing trend in communicable diseases. Obviously, the health problems erode the wealth of rural India. Special emphasis is necessary to bring about some kind of equality and justice in the matter of health facilities and infrastructure. Hence, special consideration should be given to rural health to bring them on par with the urban population. The following areas are important to achieve better health in the rural areas.

1) Overall improvement in living environment including availability of safedrinking water, essential food articles and sanitational facilities.
2) Health education to create better awareness among the people about all aspects of healthy life.

3) Removal of illiteracy and bridging the information gap between rural and urban people. A health information revolution is essential in rural areas.
4) Higher allocation of funds to rural health sector to bring equality between the per capita health expenditure of rural citizen and urban citizen living at the lower and higher strata of the society, respectively
5) Integration of various aspects of rural health such as malnutrition, education, improvement of living conditions, etc., to bring about positive changes in the health condition of the rural people.
6) Total dedication, humanism and scientific innovation in implementing health programmes.
7) Monitoring and assessment to ensure that the entire funds allocated for each project are spent correctly.
8) Establishing hospitals with latest equipments and facilities and experts in the field for the benefit of the rural people.

In a nutshell, it can be said that the health services required by rural population is quite different from the urban people. The Integrated Health Programme for the rural sector will have to be formulated keeping in view the backwardness, low level of living standards, malnutrition, illiteracy, low income and the present availability and accessibility to health services. All these years, there have been increased emphasis for urban health both in the government and private sectors. Now, it is necessary to shift the emphasis from the urban to the rural areas keeping in view the multifaceted health problems prevailing there and the importance of their potential for national development.

The Basic Minimum Services (BMS) launched by the government in 1996 envisaged the following:

a) Hundred per cent coverage of provision of safe drinking water in rural and urban areas.

b) Hundred per cent coverage of primary health services facilities in rural and urban areas.

c) Universalisation of primary education.

d) Provision of Public Housing Assistance to all shelterless poor families,

e) Extension of the midday meal programme in primary schools of all blocks and urban areas.

f) Provision of connectivity to all unconnected villages and habitations, and

g) Streamlining of the Public Distribution System with focus upon the poor.

If the above minimum basic necessities are implemented in all rural areas, it will go a long way in tackling the health problems of the rural population.

Thus, the improved health of the poor and rural people is very important for all developing nations. The explosion of knowledge and medical facilities in the second half of 20th century will be beneficial to the poor and rural people in the 21st century, only if there is humanism and scientific innovation, equality and justice in providing health facilities to them. According to *Human Development Report 1998* the 20th century's explosion in consumption has brought immense benefit to humanity, greatly advancing human development. But it has largely bypassed many of the world's poorest people. Inequalities are growing and the natural systems on which all people depend are more endangered. There should be some equality in the consumption pattern and health and medical services. Then only will the developing countries benefit from the advancing human development. Let us remember that rural health is very important for national progress, as the village people constitute the majority in our population. This is true of any developing nation.

Role of Government and Various Agencies in Promoting Health

Various agencies and government will have to play a key role in promoting health.

Government

Government policy, legislation and support are essential to improve the living conditions of the rural and tribal people. Government support is necessary to prevent and control diseases. The following areas need government support and assistance:

1. Formulating clear health and housing policies for poor.
2. Sufficient health workers, hospitals and health centres.
3. Measures aimed at giving clean water supply and sanitation.
4. Proper standards and codes to control pollution.
5. Effective machinery for health education.
6. Sufficient waste disposal system.
7. Sufficient food supply to poor people.
8. Prevention of malnutrition in women and children.

Family

The head of the family will ensure proper care of the living conditions at home. The following areas are important.

1. Planned and proper utilisation of income.
2. Better care for women and children.
3. Ensure family food, water and healthy home environment.
4. Proper health care to family members including immunisation of children.
5. Seek community support and assistance when needed.
6. Prevent home accidents.

7. Promote cleanliness at home.
8. Provide food to meet nutritional needs of family to prevent malnutrition.
9. Cultivate kitchen garden and poultry rearing
10. Adopt healthy hygiene habits.
11. Make home a safe place to live in.
12. Recognise the early signs of disease and provide timely treatment.

Community

The role of the people and the community is very important. Without community participation, better living standards cannot be attained. Actually, the community is partner of health care. Special attention is necessary in the following areas.

1. Inform and educate families on health care.
2. Remove prejudices and stigma attached to various diseases. This will help early detection and treatment of the case. This will prevent spread of the diseases.
3. Effective use of grassroots level health, personnel, schools, religious places and homes for the promotion of better health.
4. Prevent water contamination and ensure clean drinking water, possibly through community water supply system.
5. Prevent pollution and health hazards in common places.
6. Construct latrines, drains and initiate action to remove wastes.
7. Establish community centres for health education.
8. Form pressure groups to help the people in health care.

Voluntary organisations

Non-governmental organisations are required to play a key role in promoting health care. They can do a lot of work in partnership with the government and the people. The following areas are important:

1. Non-formal education
2. Survey for immunisation, early detection and treatment of diseases.
3. Organise radio, TV programmes, seminars and meetings to promote health education.
4. Organise free medical camps for poor people.
5. Rehabilitation work.

The role of voluntary organisations in preventing and controlling diseases are well recognised today. They have to play a key role in promoting healthcare projects. They have to work in partnership with the government and the community. They have to be instrumental in health education.

Thus it can be seen that the individual, family, government, community and voluntary organisations will have to play a key role in promoting health among the rural people. This will help to prevent diseases and give a healthy life to the people.

12

The Need of the Hour

> The continuing armed conflicts and nuclear proliferation, the worsening environmental degradation, population explosion with associated socio-economic problems, deepening poverty and ever-widening socio-economic contradictions, the relentless attack of new generation diseases, and erosion of moral, social, educational and spiritual values have started to weaken the foundation of human civilisation. If we fail to understand the reality and act swiftly, we may not be able to prevent the impending catastrophe. Hence the need of the hour is a great creative effort born out of every educated and intelligent man to save the sinking human civilisation.

The challenges ahead are formidable. Unless there is a uniform thinking and dedicated work with oneness of purpose, we may not succeed in our endeavour. We must work with social consciousness and sincerity to convert every mind into an intelligent and working mind capable of understanding the realities of human problems. Then only will we be able to strengthen the base of the social structure and provide the right leadership to enter into an era of peace and prosperity.

The imperative need for great creative efforts born out of reason, intelligence and hard work has become inevitable to save the human race from self-destruction and degeneration. It is certain that unless the increasing anti-social, inhuman and disastrous events are averted, unless some rigid control is imposed to prevent continuous assault on natural systems, unless the degeneration of human values is arrested, barbarism and arrogance, which were buried by the appearance of science and education will again forcefully attack man. As a result, there will be widespread human rights violations, and chaotic social, economic and political conditions, the ultimate result of which will be degeneration and destruction. There is, therefore, an urgent need to restore human values, brotherhood and tolerance in society as a preliminary step to create a world where even the poorest of the poor will live without fear and without hunger.

If the present trend is allowed to continue, it will encourage growth of selfishness, indiscipline, hatred, cruelty, exploitation, corruption, inequality and injustice. Needless to say that its undue influence on man will destroy the civilised social order and values in society. In such socio-political conditions, there will be dispersal of will and intelligence towards destruction. The world is today dominated by destructive activities on the one side, and attack of diseases, poverty and poor living conditions on the other. The victims are often the majority poor people living in the lower strata of the society. We can save the victims only by promoting human love, brotherhood, truth and tolerance. The well-being and progress of each and every human being should be the responsibility of all, in a civilised and progressive world.

We should, therefore, promote and strengthen the pursuit of human love and brotherhood through social, economic and political equality and justice. As a first step in this direction, we should bring to light the cosmic greatness of Hinduism, the truth of Buddha, the spiritual foundation of Jainism, the wisdom of Christianity and the spiritual standards of other religions. This will promote infinite love and brotherhood, and the concept of *oneness* of man in society irrespective of creed, religion or caste of the people.

To achieve this goal, there is need for a change in the mind and outlook of man—a change for a better future of mankind. At this stage, a change of mind, change outlook, change in behaviour and a change in the relationship between man and man is indispensable to face the challenges of self-destruction in the new age. A world political or economic order without peace, harmony, brotherhood and cooperation will not help to save man from the dangers hanging over his head. There is an imperative need for a social, moral and spiritual awakening to create a favourable environment for peace and progress in society.

Education in the eyes of futurologists is a failure today. It has not helped man to understand the feelings and importance of people living at the bottom of the society. It has not helped to remove barbarism and inhuman activities from the society. It often promotes a negative attitude rather than a positive one. It has given importance to the present ignoring the future. In view of the limitations of education, it has not helped man to fully equip himself and face the challenges of the future. The main objective of education today is to satisfy the ego for a job. It has not done anything substantial to strengthen human values, brotherhood, tolerance, truth and a broad outlook in man which are essential to save the world from destruction. The growing rebellious, crazy, cruel and inhuman behaviour prevailing in society will do more harm than good for the future society. A broadbased education is necessary to root out these behavioural trends and save the future generations from degeneration. In other words, the need of the hour is a result-oriented educational system that will produce a community which can save future man from self-destruction. The goal of education should be to create a safe future for man.

Human life is sacred. The socio-political environment should help the future society to preserve the dignity and honour of every human life and protect his right to live without fear and hunger, intellectual freedom and civil liberties. The development should not be at the cost of the poor people but they should be made partners of development enjoying its benefits with equality and justice. This is an essential requirement of future man. It should be the goal of education. The quality of thinking, the quality of life of every citizen and their peaceful coexistence is necessary for a progressive socio-economic environment in human society.

The world is today crying for a new social order where the victims of war, exploitation, poverty, unemployment, abuse and violence can live a peaceful life without fear. In the present-day environment, the tremendous advance in several fields increase the problems of common man. As a result, the more the man advances, the more are the problems in society. Hence, the majority of the people are not able to benefit from the advances and progress. On the country, these people fall victims to unsurmountable problems, which make their life miserable and death threatening. This gives us an opportunity to assess the progressive quality of our present civilisation and its ability to share the benefits of development equitably with the entire mankind. In other words, it reveals the inability of the present civilisation to protect the suffering people of the earth from poverty, fear, diseases and destruction. It will also reveal the absence of 'will' in the progressive world to help the poor people. Hence, the question before these people is whether the present civilisation is for self-destruction or survival. The achievement of mankind is meaning less to the large number of people who are not benefited by it, who are not able to come up in life in spite of the progressive trend the world over. It is therefore, indispensable that the fight between man and man, between one community and another, between one nation and another and between one group of nations and another should end forthwith. And the responsibility of rescuing millions and millions of people living at the bottom of the society should be taken up immediately by the progressive world. The target of all progress and advance should be the well-being of mankind as a whole and not this part or that part of the world. Such an outlook alone can create a safe and progressive future for man.

If this is not done, the nuclear weapons, diseases, poverty and environmental calamities will wipe out the human race. Relevant here are the views of Sir Kingley Dunham contained in his article titled "Our Plundered Planet:" If man's days are numbered, it is his own fault. If there was anyone left to write the history book the cause of the end of the human race could be summed up as the result of greed, thoughtlessness and carelessness. Nothing grandeur than that."

Therefore, a change of consciousness is a necessity for future unity and survival of man. Significant in this context is the message of the mother of Auroville reflecting the vision of Sri Aurobindo, which explains the necessity for such a change: "The future of the earth depends on a change of consciousness. The only hope for the future is in a change of consciousness and the change is bound to come. But it is left to men to decide if they will collaborate for this change or will it have to be enforced upon them by the power of crashing circumstances."

It is for this change that we need a great creative effort. It is this change that we need to save mankind from destruction and help every human being on earth to live a peaceful and progressive life with equality, justice and opportunities to grow in line with the changing times.

The great advance made by science has taken man to the threshold of an age of tremendous material growth. But in spite of the wonderful scientific and technological advancement, atleast half of the population is at the bottom of this growth. They are sinking every day. And to them are added many more year after year. Today human civilisation for these millions is a sinking ship. Erosion of moral and social values, huge economic waste and struggle of thousands of millions of people for existence at the bottom of the human civilisation make it a wrecked ship slowly sinking. It is because of this that the question of self-destruction or survival arises today. It is because of this, that we need great creative efforts to save mankind from destruction. This can be achieved only if we change our attitude towards the poor people, the downtrodden, the voiceless and village people, who are born to live in poverty and misery. The fact that they are in millions covering about half of the population of the world makes our task a formidable and challenging one. We can save them and give them a progressive life only if we restructure our civilisation on the pillars of equality, justice, liberty, fraternity and opportunity. This restructuring at the dawn of the new century will change the life of these poor and voiceless people for the better.

13

The New Millennium Prayer

The advent of the new millennium is a great event in human history. The occasion was celebrated with great joy and enthusiasm. On that auspicious moment, everybody would have prayed for their own health and happiness. Perhaps, a few community prayers were also held in different parts of the world. But, few would have prayed for the well-being, peace and prosperity of the whole mankind. We must realise that the individual is an integral part of mankind, and that the health and happiness of the individual depends on the peace and prosperity of the whole mankind. Hence, every individual should work with devotion to promote peace and prosperity of the whole mankind. This can be achieved only with a change of consciousness. Our new millennium prayer should, therefore, be for a change of consciousness, which is the one and only way to promote peace and prosperity for mankind.

At the stroke of the midnight hour, between a few seconds of 31 December 2000 and 1 January 2001, the third millennium was born. The birth of the new millennium was celebrated with great joy, enthusiasm and spirit all over the world, as the global media projected a new millennium image everywhere. It was indeed a landmark in human history and on that auspicious occasion, prayers were held all over the world. Everywhere people prayed for their own well-being and prosperity; perhaps a few community prayers were also held.

On that historic occasion, perhaps, few would have prayed for peace and prosperity of the entire mankind. Few would have prayed for the well-being of the people of their own country. We should not forget that we are part and parcel of mankind, and what is happening in society is bound to affect the life of each and every individual. Similarly, the thinking and action of the individual is bound to influence the progress or otherwise of the society. In other words, the safety, security and prosperity of mankind is a reflection of the well-being of the individual. But a majority of the individuals are not happy. Most of them are living in miserable conditions.

Hence, we should have prayed from the core of our heart for the well-being, peace and prosperity of the entire people of the world. In order to understand the inseperable relationship between the individual and the society, the observation of 1. Frolov in his book *Global problems and the future of mankind* is an eye-opener to us: "Each man is an integral part of mankind—this truth was perhaps never preserved as sharply as it is in our own times. He is part of all of mankind both in life and in death. This is why individuals cannot have a future that is distinct of all humanity, while the destiny of mankind itself is inseperable from that of each individual; it is also his own destiny."

Hence, we must realise that we are part of mankind. Our life is controlled and governed by what is happening in society. In this light, our prayer for our own well-being, peace and happiness, may not do any good, if what is happening around us in human society is unhealthy and unfavourable. So, it would have been more appropriate for us to pray, individually and collectively, for peace and prosperity of the mankind as a whole. But even now it is not too late, as the spirit, enthusiasm and momentum of the new millennium celebrations have not yet died down. We must therefore pray for the peace and prosperity of the entire people of the world.

What is important to remember is that no individual, no family and no country, however much powerful it be, would not be able to live in isolation. In the present day world, whether it is the individual, the family or the nation, they are inter-dependent in all matters including safety, security, peace and progress. In a democratic society, the welfare of the individual is the responsibility of all and the welfare of the mankind is the responsibility of the individual.

The new millennium is born with over a million problems and challenges. Thus the six thousand million people in the world have six thousand million problems or more. The challenges before mankind are formidable and each and every individual has to work unitedly to face the challenges with courage and determination. Hence, we should now pray for the well-being of the entire mankind and promise our capacity, our resources, our wisdom, and our experience for the benefit of mankind.

In our new millennium prayer we should honestly pray for a change of consciousness. Such a change in our consciousness alone can stop the cruelties and crimes being committed against innocent people and children. A change of consciousness is indispensable to find lasting solution to the problem of nuclear proliferation and the threat of annihilation.

A change of consciousness is indispensable to bring about a change in the attitude, in the outlook and in the behaviour of man. This will pave the way to restore confidence and strengthen understanding, and improve the relationship between man and man, man and environment and between nations. Again, a change of consciousness is *sine quo* non to make the principles of love, brotherhood, and tolerance acceptable to all nations of the world. A change of consciousness is essential to restore the lost glory of human values. In a nutshell, our new millennium prayer should be for a change of consciousness, as such a change alone can bring peace and prosperity to the entire mankind.

A change of consciousness is inevitable for every child, man and woman to face the highways and byways of modern life with courage and confidence. The challenges of peace and disarmament are formidable but that has to be met at all cost for the sake of future human survival. Nuclear proliferation and the indiscriminate use of weapons may destroy mankind and nature at any time. It is to prevent such a thoughtless, selfish and suicidal act of man that we need a change of consciousness. There is no denying the fact that in spite of our highest civilisation and marvellous progress, we are still following the 'might is right' attitude of our ancestors.

In the third millennium, we should not show our might by killing the innocent men, women and children, who are the most unconnected people. Needless to say that such an act is below the dignity of man and his present civilisational status. Neither the Almighty nor any power on earth has authorised such mass killing of people to settle disputes between rulers of two or more nations. In this civilised world, there should be no more nuclear proliferation, development and use of nuclear and chemical weapons, and there should be no more use of weapons to destroy mankind. Instead, there should be a strong bond of friendship paving the way for total harmony in the world. Such an atmosphere alone can save mankind from self-destruction. It is to achieve this goal that we need a change of consciousness.

Hence, using the highest level of civilisational values, using the benefits of education and other achievements, we should enforce a code of conduct to stop all aggression, wars and use of weapons. Our effort should begin with a moratorium on nuclear weapons. We should write the history of the new millennium in the language of peace and disarmament. We must realise that our duty and responsibility is to protect human beings and not to destroy their God-given opportunity to live as a human being. The highest function of a civilised mind, an educated mind, and a progressive mind is to understand his fellow beings and respect values in society. In order to achieve this noble goal, we need a change of consciousness and our new millennium prayer should be to realise this dream.

A change of consciousness is also necessary to fight for equality and justice, undo the widening socio-economic, contradictions, remove poverty and hunger and improve the quality of life of the majority people in the developing world. We are proud that we are now in the highest peak of civilisation. We are proud of many achievements to improve the living standard and our status. We are proud that we have achieved many milestones to increase food production. And how many people in the world are enjoying these benefits? How many people are with us in the highest peak of civilised circle? To get a clearcut answer to these questions, we should do self-questioning.

A recent FAO report indicates that about 840 million people (equivalent to the population of US, Canada, Europe and Japan), out of the total estimated world population of 6,000 million, go to bed with an empty stomach. And according to the World Bank Projections, there are about 1.3 billion people below the poverty line with an income less than $1 a day. And, surprisingly, in the world of plenty, at least there are some, who depend on dumping grounds for livelihood. Paradoxically, global statistics indicate that about 30 people die of poverty every day and half of them are infants and children.

The UN Report that the richest 20 per cent of the world's population consume 86 per cent of the world's resources only indicate the low standard of living of the 80 per cent of the population who share the remaining 14 per cent of the resources. This is a grave inequality and injustice in our civilised world. If we fail to undo these inequalities, it would reveal that our talking of democratic values have no meaning, our development have no socialistic spirit and our education have no influence on man.

Hence, the new millennium gives us an opportunity to bring about a change in living pattern and help the majority poor people to improve the status of life by sharing the benefits of development and democracy. And it is for this, we need a change of consciousness, a change of outlook. So, we must pray for a change of consciousness to save mankind from poverty and hunger. In this regard, let us keep in mind the warning of the President of the World Bank, Dr. James Wolfensohn: "if the world cannot make progress against hunger and poverty by the year 2025, there could be four billion people living on less than US $2 per day and more than 2 billion living in extreme poverty."

Now it is an opportune moment for us to realise the seriousness of the situation and work with total dedication to put an end to poverty and hunger in this world of plenty. A change of consciousness is the most important factor to achieve success in this direction.

A change of consciousness is very necessary to save the natural resources and environment from destruction and degradation. If the environmental degradation and destruction of nature is not stopped forthwith, the consequences of the impending disaster will be unbearable to mankind. We must, therefore, change our attitude, and our behaviour to protect nature. Our education has not taught us the truth that nature is life. Our experience has not taught us that environmental degradation is dangerous to mankind. So we must now learn the relationship between man and nature, and change our attitude and behaviour towards nature.

Nature and man are inseperably connected and one cannot live without the other. Here, the words of Marx will help us to change our attitude towards nature: "Man lives on nature—means that nature is his body with which he must remain in continuous interchange if he is not to die . . . .Society is the complete unity of man with nature—the true resurrection of nature—the accomplished naturalism of man and the accomplished humanism of nature."

From the above observation, it is clear that man is fully dependent on nature. Man and nature are inter-dependent. It can be said that life is nature and nature is life. So, if man destroys nature, it is bound to retaliate. We must, therefore, live in harmony with nature. But this is possible only if we change our attitude and behaviour towards nature. This can be achieved only with a change of consciousness in man. We should, therefore, pray for a change of consciousness.

Our progress and future survival depends on education. The mental, physical, intellectual, spiritual, cultural and social development of man depends on the quality and variety of education. So, the quality of education is important in shaping a better future for man. This goal can be achieved only with a total change in the objective and purpose of education. In a democracy education is very important to bring about over all development and improvement in the quality of life.

Any democracy dominated by problems of deprivation, disparities and contradictions, can change and give the benefits of development to people only with the right type of education. Here the observation of Subash C Kashyap in his book *Citizens and the Constitution* is worth remembering: "The whole edifice of democratic society is built upon mature, conscious, responsible and rationally thinking individuals. This is possible only through proper education and the inculcation of democratic values, work ethics, civic sense, patriotism, personal integrity and feeling for fellow citizens. Education for democracy, therefore, becomes a moral enterprise. Apart from education for democracy, we need education in democracy. Democratic institutions and processes themselves need to be studied and appreciated."

In a nutshell, the success of democracy depends on the interest, public spirit and civic sense of citizen. We should re-orient our educational system to achieve this goal. Needless to say, a change of consciousness is very essential to make the role of education effective and result-oriented in our democracy. Our millennium prayer should therefore be for a change of consciousness.

Today, the benefits of development are not within the reach of people at the lower strata of the society. Even today equality and justice still remain a dream to the majority poor people. We should, therefore, extend the benefits of development to the poor people and only then can we achieve the constitutional goal of equality and justice and expedite the tempo of development. In this context, the observation of Dr. B. R. Ambedkar in his speech at the Constituent Assembly on 25 November 1949 is an eye-opener to all of us.

> "We must make our political democracy a social democracy as well. Political democracy cannot last unless there lies at the base of it social democracy. What does social democracy mean? It means a way of life which recognises liberty, equality and fraternity as the principles of life. These principles of liberty, equality and fraternity are not to be treated as separate items in a trinity. They form a union of trinity in the sense that to divorce one from the other is to defeat the very purpose of democracy."

A change of consciousness at all levels will only bring changes in the working of our democracy making political democracy and social democracy two wheels of development.

Children are said to be the asset of a nation. But today a majority of the children are living in dangerous, unstable and miserable conditions. It is said that an undeclared war has been going on against children. Perhaps, the greatest crime of man during the 20th century was committed against children.

The future of mankind would depend upon what provisions we make for today's children's progress. So, our attitude and behaviour towards children and their development must change. We must work hard to give better education, better qualities, better values better character and health to all children. The present trend of childrens' over-exposure to TV, fashions, advertised consumerism, modern lifestyles associated with drugs and alcohol, etc., is dangerous. Such habits, which evaporates their hidden potential and drains their valuable energy, will do more harm than good to them. It will adversely affect their future and the future of the nation. So, we must de-addict them from such undesirable habits and make them concentrate on their education and development. A change of consciousness alone will help us to change our attitude and behaviour towards children and their development.

In a nutshell, every man needs a change of consciousness. We need it to perform our duty with devotion, honesty and integrity. We need it to shoulder our responsibility and accountability with a sense of humanism and perfection. We need it to put an end to the unthinkable cruelty to nature and man, to end killing of man by man, to end poverty and hunger, to understand our fellow-beings and promote brotherhood, and to establish a clean and corrupt-free democracy everywhere. A change of consciousness is imperative to promote brotherhood, tolerance and understanding between nations and to end nuclear proliferation. Again, we need a change of consciousness to change our lifestyle and prevent diseases. In a nutshell, a change of consciousness is indispensable for the future survival of mankind. Here, we must imbibe the spirit of the message of The Mother of Auroville reflecting the vision of Sri Aurobindo:

> The Future of the Earth depends on a change of consciousness. The only hope for the future is in a change of consciousness, and the change is bound to come. But it is left to man to decide if they will collaborate for this change or it will have to be enforced upon them by the power of crashing circumstances.

At this late hour of the new millennium celebrations, let every child, man and woman pray for a change of consciousness, as a change of consciousness is the only way to escape from total annihilation and achieve the goal of peace and prosperity in the world.

14

Relevance of Spiritual Brotherhood in Modern Times

The government of all countries, irrespective of the system of governance and the people the world over, irrespective of their caste, creed, religion, language and such other social, political and cultural variations, should forget their differences and come together to meet successfully the challenges of survival in the new age. They should come together, work together and march forward as one people one world with determination and foresight to drive away all forces destroying the human civilisation. This will help to put an end to all wars, violence and conflicts and to remove the fear, hatred and frustration from the minds of the people. Then only can we establish an era of peace and prosperity giving the benefits of development to all people. This should be our vision and our goal for the 21st century.

The initiative for this journey should come from each individual. The journey should begin immediately, as there is no time to lose. But this is possible only if we sow the seeds of spiritual brotherhood in man to strengthen the feeling of oneness and universal brotherhood, fraternity, friendship, tolerance and cooperation, which are indispensable to move towards our goal.

Hence, the first and most important task of man in the new millennium is to recognise the *Oneness of Man* and to unite as one people to meet the challenges of survival and save mankind. In this light the following observation and preachings of one of our ancient religious pandits will be a source of inspiration to us: "The spiritual visions of man confirm and illumine each other. We have the cosmic greatness of Hinduism, the moral issues of Zoroaster, the joy in the truth of Buddha, the spiritual victory of Jainism, the simple love of Tao, the wisdom of Confucius, the poetry of Shinto, the one God of Israel, the redeeming radiance of Christianity, the glory of God of Islam, and the spiritual vision of man come from One Light. In them, we have lamps of Fire that burn to the glory of God."

Let the people of the world imbibe the spirit of this message and unite spiritually, socially, emotionally and culturally as 'One People' to fight against the enemies of human progress and establish an era of peace and prosperity.

In a nutshell, in future, we should be guided by a golden message in the Tamil Classics which spoke at such a hoary past about the brotherhood of man:

> "Every country is my country; Every man is my kinsman"

The relevance of spiritual brotherhood in modern times is gaining momentum, as the classes and divisions increase alarmingly. The divine thread connecting mankind has considerably weakened in today's society. As a result, the moral law is weakening, moral values are degenerating and the human mind losing its power and sacredness. The wars, merciless killings, conflicts, confrontation, frustration and selfish aggression are all caused by the breakdown of the spiritual unity of man. This situation has created a crisis in every mind, in every family and in every country and there is increasing hatred, violence, indiscipline, intolerance and exploitation in our society. If we fail to reverse this situation, life will become impossible on earth. The only way to reverse the worsening situation in human society and to save mankind from destruction is to strengthen the spiritual brotherhood of man.

Human society today is full of classes and divisions based on caste, sect, creed, race, religion, language, regional and political ideologies. These classes and divisions are often the enemies of mankind's progress and prosperity. It has created a serious crisis in the interpersonal relationship of man the world over. As a result, life today is a struggle of man against man; the more divided we live, the quicker will be our fall. As a result of the increasing disintegration, selfishness and disunity, challenges and problems are increasing day by day, and being formidable they can be successfully met only by the united efforts of man. We should all come together and work together as one force to achieve development. The revival and strengthening of the spiritual brotherhood of man is indispensable and imperative to remove indiscipline, mistrust, hatred, selfishness and other evil spirits from the mind of man and to strengthen the spiritual thread connecting mankind. So, there is great relevance to the spiritual brotherhood of man in the modern age. We have to accept the spiritual truth for future survival and progress. If we want to give the benefit of peace and development to each and every human being, to every family and to every country, we should abide by the moral law and the spiritual truth.

Today, spiritual brotherhood is essential to promote friendship, tolerance, cooperation, non-aggression and peaceful coexistence, which are indispensable to put an end to the merciless killings, and save millions of people from poverty and hunger. Spiritual brotherhood is necessary to solve the multifarious life-threatening problems in the world and to successfully meet the challenges of development for the benefit of the poor people.

Spiritual brotherhood is *sine qua non* to prevent stagnation of progress and decay and destruction of human civilisation. The brotherhood of man is the doctrine of universal religion. The doctrine incorporated in the religions of the world are: "The unity of God—one self-dependent life, prevading all things, and binding them all together in mutual relations and dependence."

If this spiritual truth is accepted by all, then the new millennium will be an era of peace and prosperity to all. There will be equality, fraternity and justice everywhere in society.

All prophets and sons of God, all teachers and guardians of humanity are the symbol of one great spiritual brotherhood of God inspired by religions. All of them, Elders say, brought the same divine message to the world, taught the same fundamental truth, proclaimed the same changeless moral law and lived a noble and inspiring life. It is this spiritual truth and moral law of God-inspired spiritual brotherhood that we need at this hour of crisis to restore the lost values of and respect to human life. We need it to face courageously the threats of decay, degeneration and destruction and meet the challenges of survival. That reveals the great relevance of spiritual brotherhood in modern times. This spiritual truth will help us to strengthen the social values of duty consciousness, order, purity, perfection, discipline and control, knowledge and wisdom. So much so, we should accept the concept of spiritual brotherhood as an important component of our mind, our culture and work. It will strengthen the concept of universal brotherhood and unity in diversity.

Thus, as preached by Prophets, "we are all children in the Father's house, and we are all brethren of one world." As we learn to see the Divine in everybody and in everything, we realise that all is moving towards a blissful goal. Hence, man should imbibe the spirit of brotherhood for his own good and for the good of mankind. The future society should be built on the foundation of brotherhood. This is the only way to (1) prevent decay of our civilisation and remove the threat of annihilation; (2) strengthen the values, and (3) make the democratic principles of equality, fraternity, liberty and justice a reality in the day-to day life of the common man.

The Message from the Epic Literature

The invisible voice of all religions is one meaning thereby 'Humanity is one'. The message from the sacred religious books and literature provides spiritual guidance for living together. It helps to promote unity among the people of different faiths, cultures and languages. The great Hindu religious epic, the *Upanishads,* is a symbol of unity of man. It reveals that many have sprung out of the *one*. Advaitic dictum has great relevance to the subject of human brotherhood.

The Upanishadic text says: "My dear One, Reality above, was the beginning. One only without a second. It created many out of itself. Having created them entered into them." The *Vedanta* is a gateway to all seekers of truth, unrivalled tradition and heritage of religious tolerance and freedom.

Writing on the Vedic thought Ralph Waldo Emerson said: "It is sublime as night and a breathless ocean. It contains every religious sentiment, all the grand ethics which visit in turn each noble poetic mind."

Obviously the vast and varied Vedic literature gives us an insight into the mind of ancient Indian people. The divine power emanating from the Vedic literature provides a strong foundation for future peace and prosperity.

The unity of man is capsuled in the following lines of *Rigveda* (X, 191, 2, 3, 4):

> "The purpose is common, the assembly is common. Common is the mind, so be their thoughts united. A common purpose I lay before you, and with your common oblations I worship Common be your aim. And your hearts united, let the thoughts of all be united so that all may happily live together."

The message of *Dharma*, truth, love, beauty faith, self-discipline and dedication were the immortal values of ancient Indian culture. With the help of these qualities, we can keep our civilisation powerful everlasting and vibrant. It can remove fear, hatred, jealousy, ambition and selfishness—the saboteurs of human unity—and strengthen the art of living together.

Equality of man is a basic Islamic thought. According to an eminent religious writer, "Islam made perfect by Almighty

Allah is a religion of peace, love and compassion. To understand and follow it is to understand the life of Prophet Muhammed (Sal). Tne cardinal guidance for the Muslims is the *Holy Quran* and its verses which help them to regulate their lives. The foremost message He bequeathed to man was faith in the oneness of God and the equality of man which form the edifice of Islamic thought."

The sayings of Muhammed—(1) "Do you love your Creator? Love your fellow beings first" and (2) "Feed the hungry and visit the sick and free the captive, if he be unjustly confined. Assist any person oppressed whether he be Muslim or non-Muslim"—confirm the broad outlook of the Islamic thought aimed at brotherhood of man.

Looking at the religious principles of Sikh, we see that the oneness of man and brotherhood are safer with them. To put it in the words of Sadhu T.L Viswani: "The essential truth of unity is sung in the Gurubani and shown forth in the lives and activities of Gurus and their disciples again and again. Guru Nanak bore witness to the truth of unity when he sang the song of silence in his heart and breathed it forth into the hearts of his followers. The song of unity sings, again and again in the Japji. The music is the music of another land. It is the music of Nanak's vision."

Listen to the Prophet's words:

The One is the True !,
And He doth dwell in all;
In all is the Eternal One !
And again:-
Recite the One !
Recognise the One
In eye, in word, in mouth
Hold thou the One !
In sleeping remember still the One
In walking too, the One
In the One Eternal
Live thou and grow

Similarly, the Christian religion stood for human brotherhood and unity. In fact that is the divine message from the *Bible*: (1) "One is your Master, even Christ; and all ye are brethren" and (2) "Beloved, let us love one another; for love is of God; and everyone that loveth is born of God and Knoweth God", are divine thoughts from the Christian religious literature. These divine thoughts provide spiritual guidance to man to establish human brotherhood.

Again, look at the religious literature of Zoroastrianism. How clear it is about the unity of man, when it says, "If I have committed any sin against the law of brotherhood in relation to my father, mother, sister, brother, mate or children; in relation to my leader, my next-of-kin and acquaintances; my co-citizens, partners, neighbours; my own townsmen, and my servants, then I repent and pray for pardon."

The spiritual message from the *Dhammapada* of Buddhist is indeed thought-provoking. It says, "Let us live happily then, not hating those who hate us; among men who hate us let us dwell free from hatred."

The *Leviticus*—the religious thoughts of the Hebrew says, 'Thou shalt not avenge, nor bear any grudge against the children of thy people, but thou shalt love thy neighbour as thyself. And if a stranger sojourn with thee in your land, Ye shall not vex him."

Some of the commandments of Buddha will help us to remove barbarism, brutality and selfishness from our society and live together in peace and harmony. The commandments are:

Not to kill
Not to steal
Not to commit adultery
Not to lie
Not to get intoxicated

Lord Mahavira, who gifted Jainism to mankind, has the following spiritual message for the unity of man:

> Live and let others live,
> because all living beings
> have equal right to live.
> All human beings are equal.
> No one is high or low because
> of caste, creed, class, colour
> sex or appearance."

The Baha'i faith also preaches brotherhood and unity of man. It teaches that racial amity, understanding and cooperation can be achieved by strengthening human brotherhood. The spiritual message from Baha'u'llah says, "The fundamental purpose animating the Faith of God and His Religion is to safeguard the interests and promote the unity of human race, and to foster the spirit of love and fellowship amongst men."

These doctrines of the universal religions viz. Oneness with God and brotherhood of man can unite man so strongly as the rock in the middle of a sea. Each religion begins by declaring of being one with God. It ends by proclaiming the brotherhood of man. The two truths are inseparable. The brotherhood of man is implicit in the Unity of God. These broad teachings of prophets and sons of God should be taught to the children of all ages so that they can grow broadminded and tolerant. But the fact remains that our children are not aware of these spiritual thoughts of unity inherent in our religions. These teachings should therefore form part of the school and college curriculum so that we can sow the seeds of brotherhood and unity in early age.

Our Secular Heritage

India is a multi-racial and multi-religious society. From the dawn of human civilisation, India's generosity has attracted people of varied faiths, races, cultures and languages. They all ultimately adopted India as their home and beloved motherland. Thus the Aryans, Sakas, Huns, Mongols, Turks, Parsees, Europeans, etc. mixed with the indigenous elements and together constitute the Indian people of today. They taught us the art of living together as one people. They gave us a strong secular foundation. Kabir, Tulsidas, Eknath, Baba Farid and Guru Nanak all preached the essential unity of religions, different paths leading to the one and the same God Almighty. They strengthened the secular outlook of the Indian people.

Our struggle for freedom, from the 1857 First War of Independence to the Quit India Movement of 1942, was a multi-splendoured panorama of religious racial and linguistic varieties fusing into one integrated nation. Nana Saheb, Rani Lakshmi Bhai, Bahadur Shah and Bagum Hazrat Mahal, Lokmanya Tilak and Dadabhai Naoroji, Chandrasekhar Azad and Ashfaqulla, Bhava Karaque Singh and Madame Cama, Gandhi and the Ali Brothers, Pandit Nehru and Maulana Azad, Govind Ballabh Pant and Rafi Ahmed Kidwai, Sardar Patel and B.R. Ambedkar in their sacrifices and struggles confirm the secular nature of India. If we want to strengthen our secularism, the new generation should imbibe the spirit and sacrifices of the great sons of India.

The Father of the Nation, Mahatma Gandhi, always tried to inculcate this spirit of secularism among the people. His message to the people of India was, "Both Hindu and Muslim are sons of India. Our mortal mothers who gives us birth is entitled to our reverence and worship. Such worship purifies the soul. How much more worthy of our common allegiance and reverence must be our motherland then—the imperishable mother on whose lap we are born and will die? All those who are born in this country and claim her as their motherland be they Hindu, Muslim, Parsi, Christians, Jain or Sikh, are equally her children and are therefore brothers united together with a bond stronger than that of blood."

We should therefore realise that India is our home and our loyalty to motherland is supreme. We should not allow others to influence our mind on this aspect. Everyone of us, irrespective of our race, religion, culture or language is an

Indian and the feeling of Indianness should be the guiding spirit in our mind. Our own progress and the well-being of the people in our country would depend upon the spirit of being an Indian. The peace and development in our society would depend upon the ability of the people to live together in harmony.

An important feature of the Indian religious heritage is its generosity and catholicism. It is these features that has made India the abode of many faiths, races and religious groups. It is these qualities that bind India together as a nation. The bountiful love, mercy and compassion of Gautama Buddha, the noble practice of non-violence of Mahavira, the technique of Adi Sankaracharya, the prayer of Jesus Christ, and other immortal teachings of Ramakrishna Paramahamsa and Swami Vivekananda reveal the unique spiritual qualities of our culture. They all lived to teach and convince people that the ONE is the ulitmate goal of all religions. Pandit Jawaharlal Nehru once said: "India is a geographical and cultural entity, a cultural unity amidst diversity, a bundle of contraditions held together by a strong but invisible thread." It is this invisible thread of unity that still helps us to live together. If that thread is broken the nation will degenerate and perish. To avoid such a calamitous situation, we must strengthen the spiritual thread of unity in the years to come.

This invisible thread of unity was strengthened by Buddhism with its principles of love, equality and compassion. Jainism with its special emphasis on non-violence, equality and oneness made rich contributions to enrich the secular culture of India. Christian virtues of love and goodwill among human beings, the ideals of universal duty of Islam and the broad principles of classical Zoroastrianism joined the mainstream of ancient Indian culture to strengthen the invisible thread of unity.

The main task before us today is to restore the virtues of human love, brotherhood and tolerance. 'This will help to realise the importance of religion as a unifying force. If everyone follows the spirit of Indian secularism, then the individual realises that he is *one*, then the family becomes *one*, and ultimately, the nation becomes *one*. This will help to strengthen the thread of unity.

Unity in Diversity

In India, people belonging to varied faiths, races, cultures and languages have been living together from time immemorial. They have lived in one society without sacrificing their cultural identity. This art of living together is the basic concept of Indian secularism. In our country, secularism is a concept based on the actual life experience of the people. Indian secularism denotes: "Sarva Dharma Sambhava"—an approach of tolerance and understanding of the equality and freedom of all religions. Thus 'unity in diversity' is the basic principle of Indian secularism.

Our country had maintained a long tradition of hospitality and religious harmony. In the last few thousand years, many diverse people have crossed its frontiers and made India their motherland. Religious tolerance and understanding has been a hallmark of our major religions. From the time of Emperor Ashoka neither the rulers nor the people have looked upon religion as a dividing factor. They preached the message of tolerance, understanding, harmony and coexistence. Thus secularism has been inextricably connected with the progress of man. Development without secularism is impossible in India.

Indian secularism is not anti-religious or irreligious. We have a deep appreciation of the rich value of spirituality that runs through the veins of every one of us. That spirituality is the source of our moral value of our ideals and of our standards of mind. This spirituality is the nerve centre of our mind. It helps us to live together as one people in one society. We respect all religions equally. No religious community is singled out for favour or attack by state. No religious community is subjected to any disadvantage by state. The state has no religion according to the Indian Constitution. For the state the religion is a private matter of the individual. The state is concerned only with full protection of all with equal opportunities and benefits. All Indians are equal in the eyes of the state.

History has revealed that India can survive and prosper only as a secular state. India is a country of many communities. Secularism must provide the needed inspiration and strength for nation building. In every village, town, city, and nook and corner of our country, people of different faiths, races, religion, and languages are living together. Secularism is a condition of social life in our society. Any setback to this living arrangement of the people will seriously affect our progress,

It is, therefore, the duty of every citizen of India to promote the message of secularism, i.e., tolerance, harmony and understanding. The success of our development plans would depend upon the success of our efforts in strengthening secularism. This is possible only if we draw inspiration from the past and march forward as one people towards the national goal.

So the art of living together is very important today. The secular outlook is essential for our survival and prosperity. Our future endeavour should be to strengthen it. In this light, the message of Pandit Jawaharlal Nehru is a thought-provoking one: "Ever since the distant past, it has been the proud privilege of the people of India to live in harmony with one another. That has been the basis of India's culture. Long ago, the Buddha taught us this lesson. From the days of Ashoka, 2,300 years ago, this aspect of our thought has been repeatedly declared and practised. In our own day, Mahatma Gandhi laid great stress on it. We have therefore a prestigious heritage to keep up and we cannot allow ourselves to act contrary to it. India is a country of many communities and unless we can live in harmony with each other, respecting each other's beliefs and habits, we cannot build up a great and united nation."

Let these words of a great Indian be a source of inspiration to us to master the art of living together.

15

Duty, Discipline and Dignity

The new millennium gives us a golden opportunity to look back on our own past performance, correct our mistakes and plan our future. In other words, it is an opportunity for self-questioning. Even in ancient days, the duty of an individual was considered important and sacred. In the olden days, they were bound to do their duty not only for their own living but also for the good of the community. But today, let us ask ourselves, what do we do for our own good? What do we do for the good of the community?. What do we do for the benefit of the nation and the world at large? All these are important because an individual has to do his duty for his own development; he has to do his duty as a member of his family; he has to do his duty as a citizen of this great country, and above all, as a member of the human society, he is duty bound to the entire mankind. To help perform our dutiesand live with dignity, we have enough privileges and rights conferred by the Universal Declaration of Human Rights and the Constitution of India.

But due to various factors, many of us are not able to perform our duties. First of all, there are no equal opportunities for work. In view of this, many people are unable to benefit from the rights of self-protection and self-development. In a democracy there should be increased opportunities to work for self-development and for a decent living. This is the first duty of a citizen. Similarly, every individual should be 'duty conscious' as an individual and as a citizen. He should have the initiative and drive to search for opportunities to work.

In our democracy, rights and duties are inseperable—two wheels of the same cart. Hence, you will benefit from the rights only if you have opportunities to do the duty. In this regard, we should remember the words of Gandhiji:

> The true source of right is duty. If we all discharge our duties, rights will not be far to seek. If leaving duties unperformed we run after rights, they will escape us like will-o'-the-wisp, the more we pursue them, the farther they will fly.

On another occasion, he said:

> I learned from my illiterate but wise mother that all rights to be deserved and preserved come from duty well done. Thus the very right to live accrues to us when we do the duty of citizenship of the world. From this fundamental statement, perhaps it is easy enough to define duties of man and woman and correlate every right to some corresponding duty to be first performed. Every other right can be shown to be a usurpation hardly worth fighting for.

In a democracy, we are bound to remember and follow in letter and spirit the duties of a citizen enshrined in our Constitution. There is no denying the fact that most of us do not even know what these duties are! These are not being taught in schools for the benefit of future citizens.

At least now, when we are entering the new millennium, we should follow in letter and spirit the Constitutional duties and do our duties perfectly.

A look at Article 51 of the Constitution of the Indian Republic would reveal that the following ten fundamental duties are laid down there for its citizens.

a) To abide by the Constitution and respect its ideals and institutions, the National Flag and the National Anthem;

b) To cherish and follow the noble ideals which inspired our national struggle for freedom;

c) To uphold and protect the sovereignty, unity and integrity of India;

d) To defend the country and render national service when called upon to do so;

e) To promote harmony and the spirit of common brotherhood amongst all people of India transcending religious, linguistic, regional and sectional diversities, to renounce practices derogatory to women.

f) To value and preserve the rich heritage of our composite culture;

g) To protect and improve the natural environment including forests, lakes, rivers, wildlife and to have compassion for living creatures;

h) To develop the scientific temper, humanism and the spirit of enquiry and reform;

i) To safeguard public property and to abjure violence.

j) To strive towards excellence in all spheres of individual and collective activity so that the nation constantly rises to higher levels of endeavour and achievement.

Now as a citizen of this great Republic, as a civil servant, as a politician, as a nation builder, as a factory worker, and as an ordinary citizen, let us ask to our own conscience—did we perform our duties with honesty, sincerity, social consciousness and with a sense of humanism? And did we encroach on others' rights and privileges during the discharge of our duties? To these and several other questions, we will get our own answers, and on that basis, we should rededicate ourselves and perform our duties more honestly to our own self-development, to the welfare and progress of the community and the human society as a whole. We must remember that the future shape of the human society would depend upon how we perform our duties today. As a citizen, we are an integral part of the human society and we should not forget our duty to the community when we enthusiastically build a kingdom for our comfort. Here we must remember that all rights and privileges are conferred on the citizen not only for the individual development but also for the social good of the people. Relevant here is the Declaration of Universal Rights, which *inter alia*, states in Article 29(1): "Everyone has duties to the community in which alone the free and full development of his personality is possible." In a welfare state, the welfare and development of an individual is the responsibility of all.

Now let us look at the large scale destruction of natural resources and worsening environmental degradation caused by pollution and ask ourselves, did we do our duty with honesty and social consciousness? As a result of our dishonest and selfish activities, environmental degradation threatens to annihilate mankind. Now let us ask ourselves, how fair were we in protecting the natural environment ? Our failure in this regard is a clear warning for man. At this juncture, we must change the direction of our thoughts and deeds. Then only can we help mankind to survive and prosper in the new millennium.

Let us also seriously look at the plight of women and children in India, hundreds of thousands of crimes committed against women, and the continuing violence against the weaker segment of the society. Now let us ask ourselves, did we do our duty with honesty and social consciousness ?

Now let us go through the thousands of cases of corruption and malpractices appearing in newspapers and cases unreported. Now let us ask ourselves, did we do our duty with honesty and social consciousness?

Let us now knock at the doors of millions of poverty-stricken, illiterate and downtrodden people living in rural areas, slums and pavements and tribal areas and ask ourselves, did we do our duty honestly, sincerely and with social consciousness?

Thus goes the long list of questions that can be asked to our own conscience every day. And each question will bring astonishing answers for retrospection. Perhaps, that may help us to recast our thinking and mindset in a new direction at this crucial moment of history.

In a progressive society, the dignity of the individual is very important. It is the dignity of the individual that helps us to measure the progress of human civilisation. In India, the preamble of the Constitution assures to secure to us:

Justice - Social, economic and political.

Liberty - Of thought, expression, belief, faith and worship.

Equality - Of status and opportunity and to promote among them all.

Fraternity - Assuring the dignity of the individual and the unity and integrity of the nation.

In a society, where justice, liberty, equality and fraternity and dignity are assured as fundamental rights, there is immense scope for maintaining the dignity of each and every individual. In such a society, the individual should be able to enjoy a minimum level of dignity. In a democracy, a standard dignity scale should be maintained to give the people a minimum level of dignity in life.

Now look at the plight of the majority people living at the low lying areas of the developing countries. The deplorable and poor standard and dignity of their life is derogatory even to the progressive human civilisation. This indicates that we have not done our duty properly. There is an imperative need to upgrade the dignity of these people.

In a democracy, rights, duties and dignity are inseperable and inextricably connected. Hence, our duty should enable the people in the lower strata of the society to avail their rights, perform their duty and upgrade their dignity to a higher level.

The dignity level of the majority people today clearly indicates that they are not fully benefited by the rights of equality, liberty, justice and fraternity. They are unable to perform their duties for self-protection and self-development, for the good of the society and mankind at large. Obviously the advent of the new millennium gives us enough opportunities to correct ourselves and perform our duties in the right manner and in a human spirit with honesty and selflessness.

Now at the dawn of the new century, let us reorient our vision, broaden our mind with compassion, love, clarity and courage, study our own past performance, recast our duty to match the democratic goals and perform our duty in the right spirit with honesty, sincerity and social consciousness to enable others living below the average level to perform their duties and to upgrade the level of dignity of the people. Our duty should help to establish an equalitarian society free from hunger, diseases, hatred, enemity, selfishness and misery.

The duty we perform should help us to achieve the goal we aim at, as the poetic lines of the late C. N. Annadurai show*:

> A world without the
> beggar's out-stretched
> palm, the miser's
> heartless, stony stare,
> the piteous wail of
> want, the pallid face
> of crime, the
> livid lips of lies,
> the cruel eyes
> of scorn,
> a race without
> disease of flesh or
> brain, shapely and
> fair, the married
> harmony of form and
> use - where
> life lengthens, fear
> dies, joy deepens,
> love intensifies, and
> Man regains his
> dignity.

---

*The goal was set by late C. N. Annadurai in his Convocation Address of the Annamalai University delivered on 18-11-1967.

Discipline is a most important quality of human mind. It is indeed the power of the mind. It helps to acquire other essential qualities like patience, perseverence, honesty, punctuality, sincerity, compassion, love and courage. This quality is essential not only for self-development but also to perform our duty in the right manner. If an individual does not have control of his mind, he will not be able to perform his duty properly. Discipline helps to establish full control of our mind and to perform the duty with excellence. So to say, in a society, where discipline is absent, people will not be able to perform their duty to enrich their own life and to establish a progressive society. In such a society, chaos and confusion, disorder and indiscipline will weaken the developmental process. So, whether it is an ordinary citizen, an educated citizen, or an organisation, discipline is most important to successfully perform their duty and to achieve the goal aimed at.

Discipline is a very important and delicate quality. A lot of practice is required to stabilise this quality in our mind. We should lay a strong foundation of discipline in children, both at home and in school. It is the foundation of the character moulded in children at the early age. This will help the child to climb the ladder of life with great success. We should watch and learn lessons from the great men who have made discipline a way of life and achieved great success in life.

Hence, duty, dignity and discipline are very important in one's life, and our efforts should be to restore these aspects of life in every individual so that the democratic principles will cherish in our society with equality, justice and fraternity becoming a reality in the life of each and every individual.

In a nutshell, duty, dignity and discipline should be a code of conduct in every individual. The efforts to stabilise these qualities should begin at the early life, so that later it will be a way of thinking, a way of behaviour, a way of work, and a way of life. This way we will be able to give dignity to every individual in our society making the new millennium an era of peace and prosperity. Social consciousness is another important factor that helps one to perform one's duty for the good of the society.

In our own lifetime, there were great men who lived for the principles of duty, dignity and discipline. One such great man was the late C. N. Annadurai who preached, practised and popularised the principles of duty, discipline and dignity to enrich life of the people. Let us follow these principles at this juncture when the old millennium ends and the new one comes in.

16

Human Rights, Women's Rights and Development

The greatest expectation of the Indian women in the new millennium would be the 33 per cent reservation in the parliament and state legislatures of India. In India, the progress of women was the central focus of the development plan during the last fifty years. In the process of development, the concept of 'Women's Welfare' in the 1970s changed to 'Women's development' in the 1980s and 'Women's Empowerment' in the 1990s. In India, where the women population is as high as 48 per cent, the right for 33 per cent reservation is a realistic and reasonable expectation.

The reservation of 33 per cent, when achieved, will be a golden chapter in the history of mankind, as, perhaps, no other country in the world would have implemented such an advanced political concept in women's empowerment. When the reservation of 33 per cent seats in the Parliament and state legislatures come into being, Indian women, would be moving close to the guiding principles laid down by the United Nations International Conference on Population and Development (ICPD) in 1994: "The human rights of women and girl-child are an inalienable, integral and indivisible part of universal human rights. The full and equal participation of women in civil, cultural, economic, political and social life at the national, regional and international levels and the eradication of all forms of discrimination on ground of sex are priority objectives of the International Community." This achievement would help Indian women to play an instrumental role in accelerating the pace of social development and becoming partners of growth and overall development.

But the millennium question before the democratically thinking people is whether the rights and privileges enshrined in the Constitution empowers women to enhance their capabilities and avail choices and opportunities in the social, economic, political and educational fronts and to play a constructive role in the total development of the nation: Obviously, enough rights and privileges are conferred on them to achieve this goal. That should have emboldened them to share equally the seats in parliament, state legislatures and provide the right leadership in national development. But this has not happened.

In this light, let us examine some of the provisions of the Constitution. Part IV which deals with the Fundamental Rights and Directive Principles contains provisions and Articles on equality before law, women's rights, etc. Article 15 of the Constitution prohibits any discrimination on the grounds of sex, while Article 15(3) clarifies that the provision will not prevent the State from making any special provision for the benefit of women. Article 42 of the Constitution provides that the state shall make provisions for securing just and human conditions of work and for maternal relief.

Article 14 of the Constitution provides that the state will not deny any person equality before the law and equal protection of law within India. Article 15 (l) of the Constitution provides that the state shall not discriminate against any citizen on grounds of religion, race, caste, sex or place of birth. Article 16(l) and Article 16(2) prohibit discrimination in general and also discrimination on the ground of sex in employment and those employed under the state. Article 39(b) of the Constitution provides that the state direct its policy towards ensuring equal pay for equal work for men and women. To further this provision, the parliament has enacted the Equal Remuneration Act, 1976 for the payment of equal remuneration to men and women workers and for the prevention of discrimination on the ground of sex against women. Article 39 (a) provides that the state shall in particular direct its policy towards security of citizens, men and women; equally have the right to an adequate means of livelihood. Article 51A(e) of the Constitution provides that it will be the duty of every citizen of India to renounce practices derogatory to the dignity of women.

But in spite of all rights and privileges enshrined and assured in the Constitution, which would bring women on par with men in all fields of human activities, and also in terms of social, economic and political status, a majority of women live far away from these rights and privileges. There is no denying the fact that a few percentage of women are equal to men in the matter of social, economic and political status. But a majority of the women are in a very low status. We have failed to give them the required education and training to enhance their potential and employment, and to improve their socio-economic status. Perhaps many of them are living in conditions derogatory to the present status of human civilisation. Hence, the plight of and the fight for equality and justice of the majority Indian women is the millennium concern today. If we want to know the realities of their life, we should go to the remote villages, tribal areas and slums and live with them for a day or two.

The National Prospective Plan (NPP) for Women 1988-2000 adopted by the Government of India points out, "Women face a high risk of malnutrition, retardation in growth and development, diseases, disability and even death at three critical stages in their lives, viz., infancy, early childhood and adolescence and productive age. In the old age, they face threats of breast and uterine cancer and menopause related problems." This clearly indicates the health status of most rural women. Even in the matter of education, female literacy is as low as 39.29 per cent as against that of male literacy of 64.13 per cent. The educational status of backward women in rural, tribal and slum areas are abysmally low.

"In India, national data estimate that a woman or girl is the victim of:*

— rape or molestation every 26 minutes.
— dowry death every 102 minutes.
— sexual harassment every 51 minutes.
— a criminal offence of torture or cruelty every 33 minutes."

According to the World Health Organisation, "Violence against women causes more death and disability in the 15-44 age group than cancer, malaria, traffic accidents and war combined." WHO studies have also suggested that between 16 per cent and 52 per cent of women worldwide were physically assaulted by an intimate partner at least once in their lives."*

A World Bank estimated that rape and domestic violence account for five per cent of the healthy years of life lost to women of reproductive age in demographically developing countries."*

According to UN estimates 14 million adolescent girls give birth each year and a large proportion of these births are unwanted. This figure does not include adult women.

All these are millennium concerns facing the civilised society. The great expectation of the majority ordinary women would be to get equality and justice in real life and to get a decent and satisfactory living standard to maintain the social, economic and health status and dignity of women. Will this be possible to them in the new century?

The new millennium gives us an opportunity to have a look at the human rights and development inasmuch as it concerns women. This point has great relevance at a time when many women are victims of poverty, gender inequality, injustice, violence, war, crimes and other cruelties, which make their life

---

Credit-Article "To love, to cherish, and abuse", by Nata Duvvury, *Humanscape*, vol. VII, No. VIII, August, 2000.

miserable. What is more and more curious is the alarming increase in the crimes and atrocities against women. The report of the John's Hopkins School of Public Health and Centre for Health and Gender Equality states that one out of every three women throughout the world have been beaten, coerced into sex and otherwise abused in her lifetime.

The inhuman brutality and torture, the alarming increase in crimes and physical assault against women including the most inhuman and barbaric act of bride burning and the ordeal which begins in the woman's womb and ends at the grave yard indicate the magnitude of the crime against women in our civilised society.

The enormous increase in the health problems of women and girls including dangerous diseases, physical injury, chronic pain, and alcohol abuse, depression and suicides, indicates the dimensions of human tragedy in our society. Paradoxically, several millions of women and girls all the worldover disappear unable to bear the violence and torture, and atleast a million children, girls and women, are reportedly driven to prostitution every year. And to most of them, life once lost is always lost. Now the millennium question is, what would the human rights and development mean to these millions? What can it do to the suffering women?

Today when we are at the threshold of the third millennium, women and girls, whether at home or outside, whether at the workplace or in the streets are haunted by fear every minute, fear of killing in the mothers' womb, fear of violence by kith and kin, fear of rape, molestation and beating, fear of kidnapping, fear of murder, of poverty, of exploitation, and fear of other social evils and prejudies. This fear of insecurity has become a part of their mind. Obviously, the situation is shameful to the civilised man. How are you going to give them human rights and development and progress?

In spite of tremendous improvement and achievements during the last 50 years, we have to go a long way to give a decent standard of living and ensure rights and privileges to women living in the lower strata of the society. Despite legislations, a large number of women are victims of violence, harassment, atrocities, rapes, exploitation, poverty unemployment and social prejudices. In spite of the dowry act, an estimated 1,00,000 crimes against women are reportedly committed by their husbands and relatives annually. Investigations have revealed that many of the deaths categorised as murders, accidents and suicides were due to harassment at the in-law's home. The bride burning practice is still prevalent in our social set-up. Female foeticide are also being reported in majority of the Indian states.

In spite of the growing presence of women in decision making at government and other levels, in various professions and enterprises, as well as in white and pink collar jobs, the majority of Indian women are trapped in the unorganised sectors of labour like agriculture, industry, and domestic, where they work in extremely difficult conditions. Low wages, unlimited working hours, no job security, exploitation, sexual harassment and lack of legal protection are serious problems haunting poor women workers. We have to go miles to bring them within the purview of human rights and development and a decent standard of living.

There is an imperative need for rigid enforcement of all Acts to prevent exploitation of and crimes against women and girls. There is also a need for new legislations, new welfare schemes and new womens' movements and a spirit of honest and selfless service to work for the development and empowerment of women. The right type of education, active involvement of women themselves and community participation are very important to achieve success in this direction. In a nutshell, our vision for the 21st century would be equal rights, and total socio-economic upliftment, health protection and political empowerment of women.

When we enter the new millennium, our mind goes back to the events of the women's movement of March 8, 1857 in which one of the first organised actions by working women anywhere in the world took place—on the day hundreds of working women in garment and textile factories in New York city staged a strike against low wages, long working hours and inhuman working conditions. Fifty-three years later, in August 1910, at a meeting in Copenhagen, the Women Socialist International decided to commemorate the strike by observing an annual International Women's Day. In 1975, during the International Women's Year, the United Nations began celebrating the 8th of March as the International Women's Day. Two years later, in December 1977, the General Assembly of UN adopted a resolution proclaiming United Nations Day for Women's Right and International Peace to be observed on a date to be chosen by each member state.

The UN General Assembly cited two reasons for dedicating a day exclusively to the celebration of the world's women.

— to recognise the fact that securing peace and social progress and the full enjoyment of human rights and fundamental freedoms require the active participation, equality and development of women.

— to acknowledge the contribution of women to the strengthening of international peace and security.

The benefits of human rights and development have not reached a large number of women in developing nations. So we have to move fast and achieve the goal set by the United Nations. The *Human Development Report 2000* states that about 790 million people are not adequately nourished, 250 million children are used as child labour, 1.2 million women and girls under 18 are trafficked for prostitution each year, 130 million people live in income poverty. The condition of majority women segment of the society is far below the normal standard of living.

Hence, the third millennium gives an opportunity to assess the present situation and plan to meet the needs of the women and upgrade their status on par with the human right and human development norms as stated in the *Human*

Development Report 2000. Our efforts should be to give to each and every women the benefits of human rights and human development. Our struggle should continue for realising and securing the following human freedoms, to enhance the well being and dignity of women everywhere:

a) Freedom from discrimination by gender, race, ethnicity, national origin or religion.
b) Freedom from want—to secure a decent standard of living.
c) Freedom to develop and realise one's human potential.
d) Freedom from fear—of threats to personal security from torture, arbitrary arrest and other violent acts.
e) Freedom from injustice and violations of the rule of law.
f) Freedom of thought and speech and to participate in decision making and form associations.
g) Freedom for decent work without exploitation.

Women's involvement is indispensable to achieve the vision and purpose of human right and development for them. The fast expanding horizons of technology, vast opportunities and change of conditions of work assure a bright future for the achievement of this goal. But what is more important and imperative is dedicated work, honesty, determination and commitment.

The words of Emma Goldman, in her essay *Woman suffrage*, is a source of inspiration to make our movement for women's development and empowerment effective and result oriented: "The right to vote, or equal civil rights may be good demands, but true emancipation begins neither at the polls nor in the courts. It begins in a woman's soul."

17

Development Strategy and Slum Dwellers

India is poised for rapid growth as the globalisation and liberalisation process moves fast towards the global economy. But what is disappointing is that in this age of internet, a sizeable urban population lives in slums and pavements. Slum population has grown at an alarming proportion in recent decades and in mega cities like Mumbai, the estimate is as high as 40-50 per cent. The grave inequality and injustice prevailing in slums is a challenge to our development strategy. The slums and pavements are increasing year after year and there is no reason why we should keep a sizeable urban population outside the development scale. As the 21st century begins, our vision should be a slum free society.

It is high time that we put the slum development on the top of our agenda. The ultimate objective should be to give these people a clean and quality life and ensure socio-economic security. There is an imperative need for a Super Express Plan to convert the entire slums and pavements into full-fledged housing colonies. The government can succeed in this endeavour if the high-ranking financial and housing development organisations provide support either by creating a special fund or adopting slums for rehabilitation. This goal is well within our reach. But there should be a political will, a change of consciousness and an indomitable spirit on the part of all. In our new millennium march towards a global village, we should not push back a sizeable urban population to live in slums and pavements at the bottom of the society. We .must remember that they are equal partners of our democracy and they have a right to get the benefits of development. We should strive hard to help them join the mainstream of our development.

Our democracy is based on the socialistic principles of equality, liberty, fraternity and justice. But these fundamental rights and privileges are not within their reach. As things stand at present, the voiceless people of the slums can never think of these basic human rights. The people living in slums and pavements are increasingly falling victims of poverty, hunger, exploitation, misery, violence and all sorts of socio-economic ills. The living conditions of the people of the slums and pavements are so deplorable that it questions the development strategy in our democracy.

This trend gives us an opportunity for self-questioning. As we step into the new millennium, such self-questioning will help to find a solution to the million problems of the voiceless people of the slums and pavements. Now let us ask ourselves, what did we do for the voiceless people of the slums? How much funds have been allocated to the development of the slums? How far have they benefited from it? How much efforts of the practitioners of democracy have been put for the welfare of the people of slums and pavements, and why are the slums growing year after year?. What is our future strategy for slums? Surly, these questions may help us to put the people of slums in our Development Plans giving them their due share of the democratic rights, privileges and benefits. That, of course, is the objective of our democracy.

If we fail to respond positively to the problems of the slums, and continue our insensitive and callous attitude, slums and pavements may grow uncontrollably, causing irrepairable damage to our democracy and creating black holes in our growing economy.

As our development moves fast on the express highway to join the mainstream of global economy, private reports indicate that, on an average, 30 per cent of the urban population lives in slums and pavements in dehumanised condition. In mega cities like Mumbai, they have been living like that on the outskirts of democracy for years. The democratic rights and development are not within their reach. There is also no serious attempt to take development to them. As such, the slums and pavements are growing and the slum culture is slowly merging with our lifestyle. This trend is dangerous and harmful to our democracy.

Slums are growing every year, as the poor, unemployed and poverty-striken rural people migrate to urban areas in search of livelihood. This has happened because democracy and development failed to give the rural people the means of livelihood and economic security.

During the last 51 years of independence, the urban population has grown from 65 million to 320 million. But paradoxically, an estimated 30 per cent (official estimate 20 per cent) of the urban population is destined to live in slums, pavements and in similar conditions. Over the years, towns have grown into cities and cities into mega cities. At the same time, slums and pavements have also been growing at an alarming rate in urban areas. There is no doubt that this unplanned and imbalanced growth of the urban sector will weaken the pillars of our democracy and cripple our development. So, there is an urgent need to rush the benefits of development to these low lying areas of our democracy to bring them up on par with the others.

There is an imperative need to study and understand the problems of these people. The quality of life in slums and pavements is abysmally low. Their purchasing power is extremely poor. There is acute shortage of work, food, drinking water, shelter, clothing and hygienic living conditions. If we can go and live with the slum people, with the people in the pavements and streets or people living in similar conditions, we can understand the sea of socio-economic problems in which they are floating and struggling for existence. We can witness the quarrels, cruelty, violence, exploitation, unhygienic living conditions, anti-social activities and wretched living environment prevailing there, where a sizeable urban population is living. Hunger in some slums is so unbearable that at times at least a few children have to depend on dumping grounds for livelihood. What is more undemocratic is that it happens when we talk of self-sufficiency in food. At a time when we talk of 'Health for all' slums and pavements are breeding grounds for all disease-causing virus. There is nobody to care for them, although they are future builders of this nation and partners of our democracy.

These slums and pavements are, sometimes, not accounted in our democracy, perhaps, for temporary slums no house number, no ration card and no identification. But still they are Indians first and Indians last. They were once our village people with great heritage who migrated to towns and cities in search of livelihood. There are a number of housing schemes in our country for upper, middle and lower middle class people. But it seems, about 70-100 million people in the slums, pavements and streets do not have any account in our housing development fund. Slum people are unable to reach a large number of loan and welfare schemes in our country. Banks write off crores of rupees as bad debts on account of people in the higher strata of the society. It appears that the people in the slums and pavements have no access to all these benefits, otherwise why should they live in an environment where no human being would prefer to live even for a day? But, they are forced to live there as these people do not have any other place to live. They are destined to live there for years. Now, in this internet age, it is not a healthy democratic practice to keep the sizeable urban population at the bottom of the society with no change. It is high time to inculcate a socialistic spirit in our development so that the people in these areas can join the mainstream of development.

That we have been giving top priority to urban development in our Five Year-Plans is evident from the development around us. But it seems that although slums and pavements are part of the urban sector, very little or no development funds have been earmarked to improve the quality of life of these people. This is evident from the appalling living conditions in these areas. In other words, the socialistic pattern of development has evaded the urban sector. Equality of opportunity in education and employment were not available to the unfortunate people in the slums, pavements and streets. This reveals the grave inequalities and injustice in our development within the urban sector.

Eviction by force is often the method we choose to eliminate slum dwellers. Of course, that is a lawful action because they are in unauthorised places unlawfully occupied by them. But there is another side to it. Such forceful eviction after years of settlement in slums and pavements obviously creates a lot of human, and life and death problems. By doing so, through a lawful action, these people are denied shelter and livelihood. After all, they are our fellow citizens, and the practitioners of democracy have responsibility to extend the privileges of democracy and benefits of development to them. All these problems could have been avoided, if we had prevented new slums developing. If there is a law for eviction after years of settlement, there should have been a law for prevention. After all, why did we allow the putting up of slums and their stay there for years, and later creating human problems by eviction. We must find an answer to these questions so that future slums can be prevented. This will help us to avoid eviction after years of settlements which would only lead to the denial of shelter and livelihood to these voiceless slum people. The slums are coming up because we have not helped them to get shelter, livelihood and economic security in rural areas. The growing slums and pavements only indicate the setbacks of our democracy in the rural areas.

The directive principles of the Constitution provide that, within the limits of its economic capacity and development, the government make effective provision for securing the right to work in cases of unemployment and of undeserved want. In a democracy based on the principles of the government of the people, by the people and for the people, there should be equality of opportunity in the matter of education and employment. It is high time for the social researches to study the growing inequality and injustice in slums and pavements, and suggest ways and means to improve the quality of life of the people living there. The problem of the slum people involving a sizeble urban population is indeed a problem of the nation. We should not allow a large number of people to live at a sub-human level. It is indeed a degradation to our democracy. At least in the new millennium we should put the slums and pavements at the top of the national agenda. Obviously, our effort should be to establish a nation without slums and pavements by taking development to these areas.

If the slums and pavements are allowed to grow uncontrollably, it will have an adverse effect on the economic scenario of the nation. At the dawn of the 21st century, we should come face to face with the dark side of our town and cities. Super express plans are imperative to reform and rehabilitate the poor people at the slums, streets and pavements to enable them to join the mainstream of Development. After all, they are our fellow citizens and as such we cannot keep them out of the development strategy.

The super express plans exclusively formulated for slums and pavements will produce tangible results only if the plans are implemented in collaboration with other organisations and the community.

The National Slum Development Plan should, *inter alia,* include the following objectives:

1) To stop the flow of rural people to urban areas by increasing employment opportunities in rural areas.

Permanent economic security to rural people is indispensable to arrest migration to urban areas in search of livelihood.

2) Converting all existing slums in the country into full-fledged housing colonies in collaboration with high-ranking financial institutions, banks, housing corporations, industrial houses, and international development agencies. Needless to say that these Institutions can contribute substantially to rehabilitate the poor people living in slums and pavements by adopting slums or creating a Special National Fund. As a social policy of their organisations, they can contribute significantly to the rehabilitation and upliftment of the slum people.
3) Provide equal opportunities in education and employment, which will, in turn, improve the quality of their life and upgrade the level of social status.
4) Prevent exploitation of slum people by vested interests.
5) Special schemes and scholarships for education of the children of the slums.
6) To convert all slums and pavements into full-fledged housing colonies.

Obviously, the pillars of our democracy rest in their foundation, which is the base of the our society. And living at the foundation of our democracy is the poorest of the poor people in the slums and pavements and rural and tribal areas. If we neglect the basic foundation, the pillars of our democracy will be weakened. In other words, if we fail to keep up the socialistic spirit in our development to improve the quality of life of the voiceless people at the basic structure of society, it may lead to the weakening of the pillars of democracy and finally it collapses.

In a nutshell, our vision for the 21st century should be a 'slum and pavement dwelling free' society. The government, the people, financial institutions and banks, industrial houses, non-government organisations and international development agencies have to come together and work together to achieve this goal through a national plan.

18

Water—Challenges Ahead for Mankind

It was at the dawn of the third millennium, the heart-breaking news about the water scarcity in some parts of India hit the newspaper headlines. In the photograph published, we saw the people running from pillar to post for a pot of water and women walking several miles to fetch drinking water. This reveals the truth that water is life and life is water. From the worsening water situation, we will be able to understand the challenges and problems ahead for mankind.

Obviously, the sustenance of life and environment fully depends on the availability of water. If there is no water, there is no environment, no agriculture, no production, no development, and no life. So, the first priority before every government and world organisations would be to make available enough water to meet the increasing needs of the people.

There is serious concern about the scarcity and security of water supplies. The availability and adequacy of water in the new millennium for meeting the needs of agriculture, industry, environment and domestic consumption is a widely discussed subject in the world today.

In every country, it is engaging the attention of the policy makers. Just imagine what would happen if there is no water at a time when we need more water for industrial activities, we need more water to boost agricultural production, more water for energy generation and, for better environment and health.

With the passing of time, water scarcity, once a rare phenomenon, is becoming a regular phenomenon. As a result of the diminishing ground water level, increasing population, over-exploitation and waste of water, and the widening gap between demand and supply, water is going to be a precious commodity in the global market.

In India, water scarcity is a serious problem. If there is delay in the onset of the South-west and North-east monsoon or the monsoon fails to rise up to expectations, water scarcity adversely affects the life of the people.

In the light of the impending water scarcity caused by drastic change in climate, failure of monsoon or other reasons, water conservation, preservation, and sustainable and equitable water distribution are becoming more and more important.

Water is a free gift of nature and is available in abundance. The surface of the earth is 80 per cent water but only a very small percentage of water is available for human consumption. According to reports, India has only 3 to 4 per cent of the world's fresh water resources. In the world as a whole and in India in particular, water availability is uneven in the sense that in some parts it is available in abundance, while in other parts, there is a scarcity. The rapid and unplanned growth of population, the growing economy, and the upgradation of life increases the demand for water in different sectors.

Paradoxically, where water is available in plenty, it is being wasted through over-exploitation and carelessness. There is no doubt that, if water is used properly and with care and keeping in view its importance for sustaining life and environment in areas where it is available in plenty, at least 35 per cent of the water can be preserved out of waste, for use at a later time. Surplus water so saved can be used through a national water grid for the benefit of others.

Over-exploitation and waste of water by individuals and community is a matter of serious concern when the nation faces water scarcity. Round-the-clock leakage in the public water distribution system, keeping open the water taps unnecessarily, and polluting the usable water are common scenes in many places. This obviously happens because of our callous attitude.

In India, the important basins like Pennar, Cauvery, Banas and the Luni are already having far less than the desired level of water. Changing climate leads to failure of monsoon or delay of monsoon and causes drought or floods. Even drying up of well is a common phenomenon in our times.

In the above situation, there is an urgent need for public awareness and public participation in water development, water distribution and water conservation schemes. Each individual should ensure that he is not using water above his requirement. Each one of them should ensure that they are contributing significantly to water conservation and preservation. Social awareness programme should be organised to educate people on the availability and future challenges of water. There should be programmes at educational institutions to make the younger generation aware of the serious challenges and problems ahead for them.

We must remember that at least half of the population in the third world countries are not within the easy reach of safe water. It is said that at least 1.5 billion people in the world are not getting safe water.

It was to highlight the importance of water that the UN General Assembly declared 1981-1990 as the International Drinking Water and Sanitation Decade. In 1993 the UN General. Assembly also called upon the member countries to celebrate March 22 every year as World Water Day. Obviously the purpose of such celebration is to create awareness about the water by giving the right information, promoting water conservation and preservation.

The media has to play a notable role in educating people on water conservation and preservation. It should form part of the National Water Policy. Programmes aimed at water saving should be organised in rural and urban areas so that a considerable quantity of water can be saved. What we should remember is that even a drop of water saved will be a precious drop to those who face water scarcity. There is no doubt that if people are educated and properly guided, they will be able to meet the needs of the people who face acute water scarcity.

According, to experts, the salient features of good water management are:

1) Avoiding waste and over-exploitation and optimum utilisation of water,
2) Conserve natural resources, and
3) Reduce pollution of water and protects the environment. Improper management of water will result in enormous proportion of human tragedy which will adversely affect productivity and imped progress.

Water situation in the world is alarming, and brotherhood, equality, fraternity, cooperation and justice in water sharing will help to minimise the problem of water shortage.

Decentralisation of power down to the panchayat level, amicable settlement of inter-state water disputes, avoiding wastage of water, mass movement to create awareness and community participation, increased water conservation, use of appropriate technology for water storage, popularising afforestation, preventing pollution of water, etc., are very important steps to successfully meet the water scarcity ahead.

Extensive research and development of cost-effective technology to convert the sea water into drinking water at an affordable cost are imperative to face the calamitous water situation of the future. If we are able to produce safe water out of sea water, it would help a lot to save mankind from water shortage of the future. This aspect of water policy should receive top priority for the benefit of mankind, and so our effort should be to develop a simple but powerful and a cost effective technology, to convert the sea water into drinking water and bring it within the reach of all on an equitable basis.

Another area of importance in the age of water scarcity is recharging urban and industrial effluents underground for using it for direct irrigation or through recharge ponds, basins, wells, etc., for agricultural use. Annually replenishable resources are assessed as 432 billion cubic meters of water (BCM). By adopting water harvesting another 160 BCM will be available.

Development and protection of vast river water potential by preventing pollution of river waters and creating a National River Water Grid to coordinate and distribute water on equitable basis will go a long way in solving the impending water scarcity. This should receive top priority in all countries, so that the consequences of water scarcity can be minimised. Storage and distribution of rain water is another area of importance to solve our water problem.

There is an urgent need for an integrated approach to successfully meet the challenges of water security. This would mean proper management, storage and distribution of surface water and ground water resources. The projects to improve water supply should, *inter alia*, include social awareness, dissemination of correct information, public participation and development of cost-effective and simple new technology.

Drastic fall in water levels in some areas and diminishing ground water level, drying up of wells, basins, lakes and sometimes, even rivers, etc., indicate the grave water situation in the coming years.

Some other solutions to water scarcity are revival of local and traditional water storage structures, innovative methods of water harvesting and integrated watershed management. Panchayate raj institutions, and the community will have to play an important role in this direction. Recycling and reuse of waste water for non-domestic purposes, special programmes for water resources protection and conservation, increasing efficiency in water distribution and use, good quality of water, drainage and control of water pollution, etc., will help to minimise the problems of water scarcity.

There is need for effective people's participation to make rainwater harvesting a part of everyday life and it will help a lot to make ground water a sustainable resource. The success of this endeavour would depend upon the public awareness about the importance of rainwater harvesting. It is a matter of concern that ground water level in some areas are falling at the rate of one metre per year. At the same time, in some other areas, it is rising at the same rate.

The following guidelines and information issued by the Ministry of Water Resources, Central Ground Water Board, Government of India, will help a lot to strengthen the water supplies and improve the overall water position through rain water harvesting and ground water recharge. The methods and techniques suggested by experts are:

1) Roof-top rain water harvesting and its recharge to underground through existing wells, or borewells or by constructing new wells, borewells, shafts or spreading basins.
2) Capturing and recharging city storm water run-off through wells, shafts, spreading basins, storm water drains, etc.
3) Harnessing run-off in the catchments by constructing structures such as check dams, percolation trenches, sub-surface dykes, etc.
4) Impounding surplus run-off in the village catchment and watershed in village ponds and percolation tanks.
5) Recharging treated urban and industrial effluents underground by using it for direct irrigation or through recharge ponds, basins or wells, etc.

The important objectives laid down are:

1) Restore supplies from the aquifers depleted due to over-exploitation.
2) Improve supplies from acquifers lacking adequate recharge.

3) Store excess water for use at subsequent times.
4) Improve physical and chemical quality of ground water.
5) Reduce storm water run-off and soil erosion.
6) Prevent salinity ingress in coastal areas.
7) Increase hydrostatic pressure to prevent/stop land subsidence.
8) Recycle urban and industrial waste water, etc.
9) Rehabilitate the existing traditional water harvesting structures like village ponds, percolation tanks, tankas, etc.
10) With minor scientific modifications and redesigning, convert the traditional water harvesting structures into ground water re-charge facilities.
(11) Use the existing defunct wells and borewells after cleaning and also the operational wells as re-charge structures.

There is imperative need for team work and leadership, public awareness and participation, public and private investment, and spread of simple technology, populariisng traditional methods and knowledge. It will help to revive and strengthen the water harvesting practices and to make available enough water to meet the future short-falls.

Successful practice of rain-water harvesting is expected to give the following benefits:

1) Rise in ground water levels in wells.
2) Increased availability of water from wells.
3) Prevent decline in water levels.
4) Reduction in the use of energy for pumping water and consequently the costs.
5) Reduction in flood hazard and soil erosion.
6) Benefiting in the water quality.
7) Arresting sea water ingress.

8) Assuring sustainability of the ground water abstraction sources and consequently the village and town water supply systems.
9) Mitigating the effects of droughts and achieving drought proofing.
10) Reviving the dying traditional water harvesting, structures and their rehabilitation as recharge structures.
11) Effective use of lakhs of defunct wells and tubewells as recharge structures.
12) Upgradation of social and environmental status, etc.

The future progress and prosperity of mankind would depend upon the availability of safe water. Water security is important for eliminating poverty, improving sanitation, health and environment and assured food supplies. Hence, water management is very important in future. Every individual and every home is concerned with water scarcity. Preventing pollution of water, compulsory water saving, preventing over-exploitation of water and degradation of ground water, are all important in this direction.

Adopting scientific methods for rain water harvesting and ground water recharge, recycling of water and revival of traditional water storing system are all important components of the future water management strategy. Public awareness and public participation are very important to achieve success in our endeavour. In a nutshell, a people's movement is the best way to achieve the goal of 'safe water for all' in the 21st century.

19

Pitfalls of a Growing Habit: From the Social Perspective

Cinema today is an inseperable habit of man. A large number of people have now made it a habit. It has become part and parcel of modern life. There are a large number of people who cannot live without cinema. There are others who are crazy for cinema. That is the impact and influence of cinema on man. But most of us are concerned mainly with its entertainment, character, sensationalism and sentimentalism. It is time for self-questioning. What do we learn after seeing a film? What values—social, educational, cultural or otherwise—do we acquire? What is its role in upgrading the status of the majority common man; most of them being permanent viewers of the movie. These are all questions relevant to our present day life. The new millennium gives us an opportunity to think about it.

Among the children and teenagers, it is a habit growing uncontrollably. Paradoxically, it often happens at the cost of their education, it happens at the cost of development. They are losing a lot of their precious time. For them, education is important, character building is important, and life building is important because it is an age for self-development. But what good they take out of cinema, what values they get from it and how much of it goes into social and intellectual development are all important questions. For them, development is more important than entertainment, as the future of mankind, the future of the world is on their shoulders.

It is in this light that we have to examine and assess the impact and influence of cinema on adults in general and on children in particular. What the influence of cinema is on social environment is also equally important, as it is a healthy environment that shapes the future of children.

The fact that children, adolescents and adults are being exposed to the same type of films need special attention. The influence of the same cinema differ greatly on children, adolescents and adults. Sometimes, a cinema, which is good for adults may adversely affect the minds of children. It may do a lot of harm to children at the tender age of character formation; mental growth and value generation. A film with extra dose of sensationalism and sentimentalism may do irrepairable damage to their mind, behaviour and attitude. They try to imitate and follow several acts and behaviour resulting in bad consequences. There are cases of violent scenes in films creating psychiatric problems in children. It may create emotional disorder in them as their mind is tender and ungrown. Such minds are easily susceptible to any violent or other criminal behaviour.

Hence, when we discuss an important topic like cinema, we have to consider all these aspects, particularly its impact on children. There are children and teenagers imitating fights and practising them outside with weapons causing serious physical injuries. There are also instances of children and youngsters, who are continuously exposed to cinema losing interest in studies, acquiring drug-alcohol addiction and imitating criminal behaviour in real life. There are also children who develop psychiatric problems after exposure to violent scenes in films requiring prolonged treatment. These are only a few instances and there is immense scope for research-oriented study on the impact and influence of cinema on children.

The new millennium gives us an opportunity to draw a line between the cinema for children and for adults. Considering various aspects, there are social reasons to keep a distance between cinema and children.

Cinema, as a powerful media, should have clear cut social, cultural and educational objectives. It can help man in attaining educational emancipation, enriching knowledge, and solving his social problems. Cinema, while maintaining its entertainment character, should not dilute its educational character. It should not exploit the weakness of man through extra dose of sensational and sentimentalism, which are harmful to children. Cinema should not harm character formation and behaviour of children. A good cinema is an asset to any adult man and woman. It can educate them, enrich their mind and shape their behaviour properly.

In modern times, cinema has to draw inspiration from our past civilisation and inculcate values in man with a view to revive the importance of it in social life. As a matter of fact, people have to learn a lot of lessons from a good cinema. A good film will serve as a source of information and inspiration to attain better standards of social life.

Cinema is an influential media. It can make a good society or a bad society. It can accelerate the pace of development, social change and educational emancipation. It can help man to attain social, moral, intellectual and spiritual development. But in order to achieve this goal, the social aspects and the social perspectives of cinema should be strengthened. A film with clearcut social objectives can be an agent of social change.

In a country with a large number of illiterate people, cinema can promote literacy. It has immense educational potential. It can be a tool to promote literacy. If used in its correct perspective, cinema can correct people instead of corrupting them, it can educate them and make them aware of their social obligations and responsibilities in society. There is no doubt that cinema with right social objectives can create an educated, intelligent and socially responsible society.

In a country, where unity in diversity is the base of the social structure, cinema can do a lot to strengthen the unity and integrity by promoting brotherhood and tolerance. It can also generate values in society, prevent its erosion and restore the lost glory of human life.

Films are said to be the first of the best media available to reform human mind and generate healthy thoughts and rejuvenate life in line with the changing times. Obviously, cinema can help us to practise democratic values and achieve the goal of an egalitarian society.

It needs no emphasis that in a society like ours which is still caught in the cobweb of prejudice, superstition, violence, hatred, selfishness, etc., cinema has to play an instrumental role to remove these social evils and recast the outlook and attitude of the people.

Inequality, injustice and other rights are yet to reach the majority people living at the basic structure of the society. The films can do a lot to educate people on democracy. Cinema should spread and spearhead the message of oneness of man to remove caste, class and linguistic tyrannies. A good cinema can also strengthen the social, moral, intellectual and spiritual aspects of life.

In a nutshell, films with social and, educational values, and with an instructive, intelligent and intellectual motives can easily bring about social, cultural and political changes in society.

In the new millennium, the vision of cinema should be a progressive society. Modern man has to learn a lot from good cinema, take many good ideas, digest many facts, and acquire knowledge. We have to ignore what is bad and harmful.

In India, cinema should project democratic values in day-to-day life and should promote equality, fraternity, justice, and liberty and guide people to establish a peaceful and progressive society.

Entertainment is the only one aspect of cinema. There are several other social and educational aspects and a good cinema should have all these features. So films should be of educational value, democratic value and entertainment values. It should bring a change in the attitude and outlook of man.

Cinema should be a friend, philosopher and guide to man. It can guide parents in the matter of child development and welfare, so that they will be able to lay a strong foundation of moral, intellectual and spiritual aspects of life in children. In a developing country, cinema has to play a constructive role in promoting health, education, rehabilitation and other social welfare activities.

Keeping in view the importance of cinema in modern times, we have to set the following millennium goals without affecting its economic viability.

1) Re-orient the social objectives of cinema and other visual programmes in line with the needs of the common man.
2) Promote unity, brotherhood, tolerance and integrity and help to achieve the goal of unity in diversity.
3) Play a constructive role in promoting education, health and dignity of life.
4) Refrain from making films harmful to children. Promote life building and character building through cinema.
5) Promote social, moral and spiritual values in society, and also social consciousness.
6) While maintaining the entertainment character, sensationalism and sentimentalism, importance should also be given to social values.
7) Cinema should aim at creating a healthy, educated, intelligent and corruption-free society.

There is no doubt that during the last hundred years, cinema has played an important and instrumental role in the advancement of human civilisation; Now there is a need to set new objectives and a new vision for the 21st century.

20

Social Consciousness and New Social Order

The world today is in need of a new social order based on Social Consciousness. This is very necessary to improve the relationship between man and man. The new social order is indispensable to prevent erosion of social values and to strengthen the moral and social foundation of the future society. Social consciousness is necessary to find amicable solutions to all problems in society. The materialistic outlook and the advertised consumerism has made man selfish and when he strives to achieve the selfish goal, it directly or indirectly affects the life of other people. It is to prevent this social disorder that we need social consciousness. If there is social consciousness in our approach and behaviour, it will help a lot to solve a million problems in our society. There is an imperative need to change the outlook and attitude towards our fellow citizens. This can be achieved only if there is a strong foundation of social consciousness in our minds. Its absence is quite conspicuous in the present day lifestyle and set-up. A new social order based on social consciousness is indispensable to mitigate the sufferings of the majority people, who are struggling for existence in the lower strata of the society. Social consciousness is indispensable to restore the democratic principles of equality, fraternity, liberty and justice in the life of each and every individual. Hence, a sense of social consciousness is necessary to give the benefits of development to the people.

Life without social consciousness will be selfish and will do more harm than good to the common man. It is only with a sense of social consciousness that we can have a humanistic touch to our work. Hence the quality of social consciousness should be an integral part of one's mind and then only will he be able to do justice to mankind. However, it is not possible to acquire this quality in our mind all of a sudden. This quality has to come into one's mind as part of one's character and culture, so that it will be a strong moral base in one's mind. The success of acquiring this social quality would depend upon the home environment, the school environment and the social environment.

But today, to our disappointment, we find that the home environment, school environment and social environment are not favourable to the growth of this quality. As a result, the quality of social consciousness is fast disappearing in our society. The serious crisis of confidence, the million social problems in our society, conflicts and confrontations, hatred and violence directed against our fellow-citizens clearly indicate the absence of social consciousness and the magnitude of problems caused by it.

The new millennium gives us an opportunity to understand the seriousness of the problem and create a favourable environment for its promotion. This will help us to become social-minded and work for the benefit of the society; and it would help us to understand our fellowcitizens emotionally, spiritually and intellectually and to help them in their byways and highways of life. It helps us to work with single-minded devotion for the welfare and well-being of mankind. It helps the younger generation to do efficient and effective social service to prevent degeneration of values and help the downtrodden and majority voiceless people to enable them to attain a higher standard of life. In a democracy every citizen is bound to follow the principles of duty, discipline and dignity which in turn helps to preserve democratic and human values in society. In a welfare state, the welfare of the individual is the responsibility of all. And the citizens will be able to follow the principles of 'duty, dignity and discipline,' only if they have a strong base of social consciousness in their mind.

So, it is vital for us to inculcate a spirit of social consciousness in children. We should create a favourable environment at home, at school and in society for the promotion of this quality in the younger generation. Today's children, being the makers and guardians of tomorrow, should have a strong base of this quality in their mind. It will give them confidence and courage to make the future a safe place for future man. It will help them to make the future peaceful and prosperous. Hence the elders of today should strive hard to promote the quality of social consciousness in children and younger generation. They should also motivate others to promote social consciousness and other social values in society.

The experience and experiments of other developed countries would reveal the significant role, this social quality has played in their progress and prosperity; nay, even our own heritage is an open book of social values, which if followed, will help us to enrich our life.

Social consciousness is essential to understand the socio-economic problems of the majority of the people living at the base of the society and to provide necessary help to them to overcome their hardships and problems. Social consciousness helps to understand the problems and feelings of others as our own and work together to solve the problems of common man.

Needless to say, social consciousness is an asset to the younger generation to conquer social evils and carry on their mission to speed up social transformation and to bring about a new social order. It helps them to stabilise other qualities like patience, discipline, honesty and sincerity in their mind. It helps them not only to enrich their own life. If we look at the present day society from a social perspective, we can see that there are neck-deep problems in our society eroding the life of most people. We cannot move forward in our development scale without solving their problems, and without restoring human values in our society. To achieve this goal, we should have social consciousness. As a matter of fact, in a socialistic pattern of society, nothing tangible can be achieved without the quality of social consciousness. People belonging to all walks of life, whether a doctor, a scientist, an engineer, a technician, a teacher, a worker or others, have to play an instrumental role in removing social evils and ills and promoting a new social order for the future. This is possible only if they have social consciousness and other human values in their mind. Without this quality, we cannot give the full benefits of our knowledge, our talents, our experience and our service to mankind.

Future man should be guided by this social quality. Viewed from the future perspectives, one of the important objectives of our education should be to inculcate human values and qualities, particularly social consciousness in children. Then only can we save future man from conflicts and self-destruction. Social awakening through a well-planned educational system, with specific emphasis on character, social and human values and development of a socially meaningful system of governance are indispensable to give the full benefits of human rights and human development to each and every citizen in our society.

Look at the killings and conflicts within the family and within the society. Look at the thousands of murders, suicides, rapes, harassment, conflicts and fights between man and man, which we are witnessing in our daily life. All these ills and evils in our society are caused due to the absence of social consciousness and other human values. The increasing habit of laughing and enjoying others' sufferings and pain only points to the absence of this vital social quality in our society. Paradoxically, the social problems and sufferings of individuals, family and the community, are increasing at an alarming rate. It is to prevent this social crisis that we need human values and social consciousness in our mind.

If we fail to realise the seriousness of this social malady silently eroding human life, that will lead to the decay and degeneration of our social structure and the ultimate collapse of the family system, the social system and human civilisation. We must immediately stop the harmful acts and cruelty being done to human beings, animals and environment. But this dangerous trend threatening the progress of mankind can be arrested only if we work with a sense of social consciousness and with oneness of purpose. Social awakening through education is indispensable to achieve the goal. So, from the social perspective, what is imperative is a mass awareness programme and social awakening in every mind. Then only each citizen will be able to play their role in promoting a new social order. We have to shape a new social conscience, attitude and outlook and this can be achieved only by people's involvement. Hard work, sincerity, honesty and unity are indispensable to move towards the millennium goal of peace, freedom and prosperity to all. Then only can the majority poor people, the downtrodden, the depressed and the voiceless get the benefits of human rights and development.

The younger generation has to work hard to enrich its mind with human values and qualities. The elders should be their friend, philosopher and guide in this direction. This is necessary to get their mind freed from disenchantment, disillusion, apathy and escapism, so that their mind can be equipped to face the challenges of social reform and social consciousness.

We must realise that whatever achievements we make during the first quarter of the 21st century would depend upon the talents, attitude, behaviour and outlook of the younger members of the society. This again would depend upon the quality of education, the quality of training, the quality of character and social values inherited and acquired by them. If we fail to give them the right type of education and training, inculcate social values and humanism and mould their character, the future of the world will be gloomy and uncertain.

The children of today are the makers of the future world. They are the future masters and leaders. They have to lead the society towards peace and prosperity. They have to lead the people towards a new social order where every human being will live without fear, sharing the rights and benefits of development with equality and justice. But this is possible if their mind is enriched by social consciousness and other human values. It is in this light that we have to understand the importance of social consciousness in our present day society. In a nutshell, the quality of social consciousness is indispensable for the future survival and progress of mankind.

21
Challenges of Globalisation

Globalisation, as an economic system, is gaining momentum in the new millennium. As a result of the tremendous development brought about by globalisation, the world is today moving towards the goal of a global village. In this age of competitiveness, the future global village is going to be the nerve centre of the economic activity. Hence, it has become expedient for each country to link its economic development to this global village. Every country will have to participate in this globalisation process to change with the changing world and to benefit from the advanced technology. Thus today, globalisation is a means to an end—the end being economic growth and development.

But for developing and poor countries, there are many challenges and problems to achieve success in globalisation. So, it is difficult to obtain immediate benefits for its majority poor population. They have to increase their efficiency and productivity through education and training. Then only will they be able to keep pace with the global competitiveness.

Some of the developing nations like India have immense potential to win the global competitiveness. India has excellent resources like talented manpower—engineers, scientists, technicians and skilled workers—who has proved their merit in developed countries. But with the same resources, we are unable to face global competitiveness. The advent of the new millennium gives us an opportunity to find out the reason for our poor performance in global competitiveness. We should find out whether it is the working environment, the low productivity, poor development of human potential or the industrial policy that slow down our competitiveness. It is high time to take remedial action so that India can play a lead role in global competitiveness. To achieve success in this direction, we should develop our human potential, and improve our quality, our talents and our ability. This will help us to increase the productivity in all sectors of the economy and move successfully to achieve the goal of competitiveness and speedy economic growth. Every citizen should play an active role in increasing the productivity and economic efficiency of the nation. And our industrial policy and economic policy should be framed to achieve this goal.

Global competitiveness is today beyond the reach of poor and developing countries. The future survival and growth of the economy of developing countries would depend upon their ability to join the mainstream of global market. It is in this light that several countries like India and China have opted for market economy. However, global competitiveness is a challenge to developing countries. The industries there should acquire dynamism and competency to face these challenges. This is possible only if these countries open up their economy for global trade and integrate it with global economy. Globalisation will help the industries to share the experience of frontliners in global competitiveness, like Japan, USA, Germany and Switzerland, and create an awakening in the industrial sector paving the way for rapid changes through globalisation. This will automatically increase opportunities for investment in technology, infrastructure and human resources which in turn will improve productivity and competitiveness of the industry.

For the industries and trading organisations in developing countries, challenges to be met are many and varied to survive and succeed in the global competitiveness. In today's competition-charged market only dynamic companies and organisations, who are willing to change and accept commitments, can survive and prosper. So, the industries in developing countries should strive to achieve this goal.

The experience of successful companies in the global market indicate that customer-oriented products, brand reputation, reliable and acceptable quality and competitive price are indispensable factors to become active players in the competitive global market. At present, dynamic and competitive industries capable of meeting the challenges of globalisation are not many. Obviously, these few industries are only benefited from globalisation. In other words, majority of the industries in developing and poor countries are not able to participate and benefit from globalisation. The reasons for this situation are many and varied. But the most important reasons can be identified as out-dated and obsolete technology, financial constrains, mismanagement and attitude of employees, low productivity, unfavourable operating environment and lack of market demand for products. There are a large number of sick industries in the small scale, medium scale, large scale and traditional sectors. Similarly, the number of industries operating with obsolete and out-dated technology is alarmingly high. In addition, there are quite a large number of industries, which are loss making and operating under difficult environment. The production output in these industries is far below the plant capacity and their products are not acceptable to the market due to price and quality factor.

Thus, the majority of the industries in the third world countries are unable to actively participate in globalisation and benefit from it in the existing operating environment. In other words, there is no equality in industrial growth resulting from globalisation. As a matter of policy, equality should be the basis of globalisation in a democracy. Then only, majority of the industries and majority poor people will be benefited by it.

In this light, the millennium question before us is, how are we going to help these industries? The matter needs serious consideration, as any delay will lead to the closure of the weak industries. There is, therefore, imperative need to study the case of all these industries with a view to make them viable units capable of facing the challenges of globalisation.

Financial assistance, modern technology, efficient management, trained and highly motivated manpower and a favourable operating environment are some of the basic requirements of these industries to move towards globalisation and a competitive market. But, this is not possible all of a sudden. Active support from Government and financial institutions and a dynamic spirit of management and employees are essential factors. As part of globalisation, there should be special programmes aimed at the viability and competitiveness of these industries. The special scheme should target each and every industry and should consider the following aspects.

1) Modernisation of the plant and technology under a time-bound programme. There should also be R&D support either individually or collectively.
2) Financial package which should include low interest term loan and working capital, exemption from duty and tax for a limited period etc.
3) Professional guidance for quality products and marketing assistance to create product demand.
4) Human resource development programmes.

There is no doubt that the Government, financial institutions and Trade Associations can guide and lead these industries towards globalisation. The management, employees and the trade unions should co-operate to achieve positive results in this direction.

But technical assistance and financial support alone will not help. There is need for dynamic spirit to make the industry self-reliant. When the whole world is changing, we have also to change. We cannot be silent spectators when the industrial economy is fast changing all over the world. These industries should be able to face successfully the challenges of the changing market with new design, product-mix, price and service to meet the customer demand.

The millennium-question before us is, when the industries in the small scale, medium scale, and traditional sectors in China, Taiwan, Korea and Japan are able to compete in the global market, why are we not able to do so? What are the factors responsible for this? How the countries like Japan, USA, Singapore and Honkong are able to become frontliners in Global competitiveness?

Thus a lot of self-questioning will help us to know the reason for their success in the global, market? And, obviously, the reason is "higher productivity" achieved through hard work. So, we must realise that we have to work with a dynamic spirit and dedication, work hard, as a team, with a commitment and then each industrial unit can become self-reliant and competitive. So to say, higher productivity is the one and only gateway to win the global competitiveness. The above will help these industries to become active players in the global market and benefit from globalisation.

Relevant here are the words of Prof. Michael Porter of Haward University who observes that the only meaningful concept of competitiveness at the national level is 'productivity'. According to Prof. Donald N. Thompson of York University, "One result of the emergence of global competition is that the factors that determine competitive position are changing fast. One of those is productivity."

The achievement of developed countries in global competitiveness and the observations of eminent experts reveal that the competitiveness of a country depends upon the higher productivity of that country. It is a known fact that the productivity level of industry in developing and poor countries is very low when compared to that of a developed nation. It is, therefore, imperative that these countries should improve productivity considerably to face the future challenges of global competitiveness.

In this light, the observation of the management expert Peter F. Drucker in his book *'Managing in Turbulent Times'* is indeed a good lesson for the industries in developing countries. He says: "There is no secret to the higher productivities. There is only persistent, hard, steady, work and a commitment to managing productivities. This commitment is now required of all managers in developed countries. To fulfil, they must set two goals in their institutions. The first is to double the productivity of money in business—the productivity of capital—within the next 8 to 10 years, at an annual rate of productivity increase of about 7½ per cent. The second is to aim at being able to produce at least 50 per cent more within the next 8 to 10 years without increasing the number of people employed; this means they must aim at raising the productivity of the people at the annual rate of 4 to 5 per cent. Both goals are attainable. Both require only hard work."

If the industries in developing countries follow the suggestion of Peter F. Drucker in letter and spirit, that will help them a lot in improving productivity and competitiveness.

The industries in developing countries should work on a firm productivity policy and increase productivity by optimum utilisation of all resources—labour, capital, machine and material—and use the gain from productivity to sharpen the competitive edge of the industry in the global market.

Opening up the economy through a broadbased economic policy will help the industries to grow in the desired direction, improve productivity and achieve global competitiveness.

In this world of rapidly changing economic and business scenario, each developing country should have a national policy on productivity, integrated to the National Economic Policy, to guide the industries towards improved productivity and competitiveness. The productivity policy should bring all the industries in the country under *Common productivity norms* making it obligatory to achieve improved productivity each year. Improved productivity should be linked to special incentives and concessions on duty and taxes so that it will be a source of encouragement to industries in this regard.

Productivity consciousness is an indispensable factor in improving productivity. Productivity consciousness of the government, management, managers and workers is very important in this direction. It was the motivating force in developed countries to achieve the highest rate of improved productivity and reach commendable heights in global competitiveness. Hence the industries in developing countries should promote productivity consciousness as a first step in achieving productivity and competitiveness.

Globalisation should generally mean participation in investment, trade, technology, transfer and selling of products and services in the global market. We have to enhance our educational, technological and industrial status so that we can increase our competitiveness. Each and every citizen and organisation will have to play an important role in achieving this goal.

But each and every country has to ensure that opening up their economy for global trade should not in any way erode their freedom, sovereignty, culture and security of the nation. This fear prevailing in some countries should be removed by progressive policies of the globalisation. The common objective of globalisation should be sharing the benefits of development on a reciprocal basis and helping the people in poor and developing countries to improve their socio-economic status. Globalisation should not lead to closure of traditional and such other industries creating more unemployment and economic problems. As a matter of policy, the advanced technology should help these industries in developing countries to increase their efficiency, productivity and growth, so that they can increase their competitiveness. Hence, the globalisation should not increase the problems of traditional industries and misery of the poor people. It should help them to improve their socio-economic status and enter into an era of peace and prosperity in the 21st century.

22

The Cyber World of the Future

The 21st century will be full of challenges and promises of the Information Age. It will affect all spheres of society, governments, educational institutions, industry and commerce, homes and citizens worldwide. Thus the advent of the third millennium has brought in an era of information society. The new era is the result of rapid changes brought about by the new technology and the cyber world. Obviously the information society offers vast scope and opportunities to human beings to identify information, to evaluate information, and exchange information for the benefits of the citizens the world over. In an information society, every human being will have freedom to land in the cyber space in search of information. Information technology is a source for total development, for improving the quality of life and for promoting better service to mankind. It helps man to be more intelligent, informative, productive and competitive in the fast changing world.

However, to be competitive and active in the cyber world, one needs to become an information literate. To achieve this one needs a lot of training, education and guidance. One should be prepared to accept the concept of lifelong learning. He should know how to organise information and knowledge, how to select and collect information, how to use the information for self-development and finally how to share information for the benefit of mankind.

This is a chain of activity and part of lifelong learning. It is therefore necessary that schools, colleges, universities, other centres of learning and libraries should train students and young people to handle information efficiently. This is essential precisely because information technology is indispensable for future survival and progress. In this fast changing world information technology is growing fast. Every minute new information is coming to help man to be more efficient, productive and competitive. The future development would depend upon our ability to keep pace with the advancing information technology.

The information society is not a new concept of the third millennium. The term has its origin in Japan. The 'Johoka Shakai' or informationalised society was first coined in Japan in the 1960's by a scientific group formed by the government. The vision of the information society is that every individual and business has access to advanced information and communication technologies. It helps them to develop their talents and potential and take advantage of the vast opportunities in employment and wealth.

In a democratic society, the main objective of the information society is to create lifelong learning habit among all the sections of the population and give information access to all and expand the public information system. The information technology should reach every home in rural and tribal areas and slums to improve the quality of life. In other words, the advancing technology should be diverted to rural and backward areas for the benefit of the majority unfortunate people living there.

The information technology provides for a new environment, new work culture, new business links and trading networks. Networked computers today control every aspect of human life. Information technology allow information and knowledge-based work to be located anywhere. It is virtually transforming and revolutionising the world.

In future, infotech will proliferate in the industrialised countries and spread rapidly everywhere else. The information technology will accelerate the technical, social, economic and cultural changes anywhere. Education experience will be enhanced by multimedia computer and other teaching tools. Global universities will enlarge connecting teachers students and researchers in many networks and other advances. Information technology will make every home more comfortable, economical and secure. As a result, the quality of life will go up. Thus, the advance of information technology will bring far-reaching changes, and promises for a bright future for mankind.

But the millennium question before us is about the promises of information technology for the majority poor people living in the bottom layers of the society. How is the infotech going to change the life of three-fourths of the world's population living in developing countries. How will the information technology help to share the benefits of development with common people with equality and justice. Will the information technology liberate the majority poor people from illiteracy? What would be the fate of these people in the information society? What would be their role in the future cyber world?

Thus challenges and problems before the planners of information technology are many and varied. It has to give education to each and every illiterate person in the world. It has to increase productivity to improve the economic status of poor countries. It has to give employment to all unemployed persons. It has to take the message of good health to all people. It should help to increase the purchasing power of each and every individual. In a developing country, information technology should help to modernise agriculture and industry.

Hence the third millennium offers vast scope and opportunities for growth and advancement. But there should be a political will, a socio-economic policy, detailed area-wise and sector-wise plan to tap the potential of information technology through all possible channels. This will help to give its benefit to the entire population with equality and justice. This will help to make use of the advancing technology to develop human potential in each country for the benefit of all. It will help us to give the benefits of human rights to all people in the country. It should help to popularise science and technology in rural areas.

Each developing country should be prepared to face the problems posed by the social and technological changes in the society. There should be well-defined and clear national and international laws to ensure smooth transformation through information technology. The future ability of an individual and the competitiveness of a country will depend upon how efficiently and effectively we utilise the advancing information technology in every sphere of human activity.

Thus the cyber world of the future will be very wonderful, interesting and very progressive. The advantages of the cyber system are many and varied. However, it has several demerits and disadvantages. The adverse changes in the behaviour, attitude and outlook of youngsters who are continuously exposed to the cyber system will be known only in the long run. From the social perspective, the disadvantages and demerits of the cyber system and the indiscriminate spread of information will be known only at a later date. It is true that the cyber system and the information technology will help a lot for the spread of information and technology which in turn will improve productivity, development, progress and wealth. But exposing children and youth continuously to the computer networks will be dangerous in many ways. It will pump in unnecessary, unwanted and sensational information into their mind, stimulating far-reaching changes in them for good or bad depending upon the influence of the incoming information. Will the flooding of all sorts of information into the mind of the young children erode the intellectual base of the mind or will it slow down the intellectual growth in children? This is yet to be known. If we pump full of information into the growing mind through the cyber system, what changes it will bring about in the intellectual development process will have to be probed. If the children and youngsters are continuously exposed to computer network, perhaps, they will not be interested in any other source of information. Again, will it create more unemployment than at present or will the unemployed workers be stranded in the cyber society? These are still unanswered questions even in developed countries. In a nutshell, the impact and influence of the cyber system on man is yet to be proved.

Hence we have to be very careful and cautious in the cyber world. The flow of information through the cyber system should be controlled and regulated through a code of conduct. There should be clearcut plans and a blueprint of the future society we aim at. The main objectives of the cyber system should be laid down and the following should be important goals for any developing country.

1. Creating a healthy behaviour and attitudes among the younger generation.
2. Intellectual development on proper lines.
3. Promoting education, training and development.
4. Use of information technology to improve productivity in all sectors, and to solve the economic problems of the people.
5. Stimulating social change and promoting social development.
6. Sharing the benefits of development with equality and justice. The development through information technology should reach the majority poor people in the lower strata of the society.
7. Preserving human values and democratic principles in the cyber society.

Care should be taken to prevent/avoid:

a) Misuse of information technology to promote crimes and destructive activities.
b) Degeneration of moral and social values leading to indiscipline and violence.

c) Crippling of behaviour and attitude of young people.
d) Children/young people becoming crazy and slaves to the cyber system.
e) Growth of unemployment.
f) Stagnation of intellectual growth.
g) Inequality and injustice in sharing benefits of progress.
h) Young people falling (1) victims of advertised consumerism and undesirable lifestyle, and (2) victims of breakdown in family system, and its serious consequences.

In a nutshell, there will be more problems, more inequality and injustice, more indiscipline and disorder in an unplanned cyber world. If the use of cyber system and the information technology is not properly controlled and regulated, that will do more harm than good both to the individual and the society. Hence there should be a clearly defined plan, and a blueprint of the future cyber world and the global village emerging out of it. The developing nations should have their own plans and programmes to land in the cyber world and to integrate with the future global village for the benefit of the whole mankind. That should be our vision and our mission in the Cyber Age.

23

The Chicago Message of Swami Vivekananda

A Call for Unity and Peace

A century ago, on 11 September 1893, Swami Vivekananda, a great patriot saint, made a 'discovery of India' at the World Parliament of Religions held at Chicago. What he discovered there was the glory of ancient cultural and spiritual heritage of India. That discovery took the assembly of eminent religious personalities and philosophers by surprise; for they never knew that such was the broad vision of *Vedanta philosophy*.

Human brotherhood and tolerance are the basic teachings of *Vedanta* philosophy. Indian culture is not just a single country's religion or culture. It is the culture of humanity as a whole. It has travelled far and wide and provided a spiritual thread for unity of man from time immemorial. This was the essence of Swamiji's historic address at the World Parliament of Religions at Chicago. It was this historic address that brought worldwide recognition to Indian culture.

The spiritual message of Swami Vivekananda conveyed to humanity at Chicago about hundred years ago, and at different parts of the world is written in golden letters in the religious history of man. The message coming as it does from the great patriot saint of India is more relevant today than at any time. The central core of his message was Oneness of Man, Religious Tolerance and Brotherhood. His spiritual message should be a guiding spirit to every man. It is a necessity to prevent erosion of values and decay of our civilisation and heritage. It is a necessity to save people from the hot furnace of violence, religious upheavals and poverty. It is a necessity to take India to greater heights in prosperity and power as predicted by Swami Vivekananda.

Obviously, the message is immortal and powerful enough to provide inspiration for human brotherhood and tolerance at all times. While talking about Hinduism before an enlightened and distinguished audience at Chicago and at other places, Swami Vivekananda was indeed making a discovery of ancient India. In his address, he traced the glorious history of *Vedanta* philosophy and the Indian heritage, and the concept of unity in diversity as practised in ancient India. To him, India was the mother of many religions, and oneness of the soul was the divine spirit to all religions. He hit out at those who were practising bigotry, fundamentalism and selfishness and said that we were all living like a frog in the well thinking that our religion was the world itself whereas the truth was that all religions were gateway to divinity and oneness. In other words, Religion is a manifestation already in man.

When Swami Vivekananda stood before the 7,000 and odd distinguished delegates from different parts of the world assembled in the spacious hall of the Art Institute at Chicago for World Parliament of Religions meet in September 1893, and commenced his speech in all humbleness as "Brothers and sisters of America." The entire audience was taken by surprise and stood up in silence. That was the electrifying effect of his message, and throughout his speech from 11 to 26 September 1893, they all heard one theme—universality of religion and oneness of man, as practised in ancient India.

We are now living in an atmosphere of fear, hatred, disharmony, violence and religious upheavals. At this juncture, if we imbibe the spirit of the few words of Swamiji—"Brothers and Sisters of America"—and live like brothers and sisters that will end all religious differences and controversy and restore the glory of the ancient heritage of India. Thus the message of Swami Vivekananda has great relevance today. His message, if taken in true spirit, will have far-reaching effect on our life in these days of religious intolerance and violence and poverty and unemployment. The spirit of that message will kill bigotry and selfishness. So much so, it is a necessity that every Indian should follow the spiritual message of Swami Vivekananda and live in peace and harmony like brothers and sisters. This will help us to use full potential of our people to establish a truly secular, peaceful and prosperous society. We should, therefore, spread the message of Swamiji for our own benefit and for the benefit of the future generation.

Here are a few words of Swamiji. He said, "I am proud to belong to a religion which has taught the world both tolerance and universal acceptance. We believe not only in universal toleration but we accept all religions as true. I am proud to belong to a nation, which has sheltered the persecuted and refugees of all religions in all nations of the earth." This message delivered at the Chicago Conference is indeed a special message for India of today. There is no need to go deep into this message to understand its close relevance to our country. We should follow it without a second thought so that we can live in peace and harmony and carry forward our heritage to posterity.

Swamiji's message also expressed concern as to how religion should be utilised for improving the quality of life and living conditions of Indian people. He was concerned with the poverty and suffering of the Indian people which he witnessed during his Bharata Parikrama. The message recognised the divinity of human beings and, therefore, the essential quality of all people and the validity of all religions, which led to the same goal of *Oneness*.

From the dawn of human civilisation, India's generosity and catholicism have attracted people of varied faiths, races, cultures and languages. They all ultimately adopted India as their home and beloved motherland. Thus the Aryans, Sakas, Huns, Mangols, Turks, Parsees, Europeans, etc., with other indigenous elements together constitute the Indian people today. This was the essence of Swami Vivekananda's immortal message to the World Parliament of Religions at Chicago hundred years ago.

Kabir, Tulsi, Eknath, Baba Farid and Guru Nanak all preached the same unity of religions, i.e., different paths leading to the one and the same God—Almighty. This was the spiritual content of Vivekananda's message to humanity.

In the galaxy of persons who preached and practised essential religious unity of man and helped to weld the entire nation into an integrated human force are Nana Sahib and Rani Lakshmi Bai, Bahadur Shah and Begaum Hazrat Mahal, Lokmanya Tilak and Dadabhai Naoroji, Chandrasekhar Azad and Shafaquallah, Baba Karaque Singh and Madam Cama, Gandhi and Ali Brothers, Pandit Nehru and Maulana Azad, Govind Ballabh Pant and Rafi Ahmed Kidwai. The thoughts and works of all these national leaders were indeed in line with the message of Swami Vivekananda. If we follow the footsteps of these national leaders who brought freedom to India, we will be strengthening the concept of unity in diversity.

Relevant here are the words of Pandit Jawaharlal Nehru: "He was one of the great founders of National Movement of India, and a great number of people who took part in the movement at a later date drew inspiration from Swami Vivekananda. Directly or indirectly, he had a powerful influence on India today. I think our younger generation must take advantage of this foundation of wisdom, spirit and fire that flows through Swami Vivekananda."

This observation reveals the relevance and influence of Swamiji's message to India of today. Needless to say that Swami Vivekananda's message will help us to redouble our efforts and strengthen our unity as one nation, one people and achieve peace and prosperity.

Swami Vivekananda predicted way back in the 1890s that India would be free within the next 50 years in unforseen circumstances. This has happened. He had made still another prediction—that India would rise to great heights of prosperity and power far more than she had done in the past. We still have to wait to see this dream of Swami Vivekananda come true. This can be achieved if we follow the message of Swami Vivekananda in letter and spirit.

Paradoxically, in our society, the difference between man and man and between religion and religion is widening day by day. The encrustations accumulated around the central core of the religion, i.e., oneness of soul, is keeping us away from the true religion, which according to Swami Vivekananda is in our own mind. If we imbibe his spirit, follow his teachings, that will help us to move close to the true religion. This will narrow down the differences prevailing in our society today. This change is essential for our own survival and for the future growth. The message of Swami Vivekananda being the inspiration drawn from the true principles of all religions will be relevant to all religions in the world. Politicians, social workers, students, the working class, the village people and all others should participate in our journey towards truth, religious tolerance, harmony and progress. All leaders of our country—political, social, religious, spiritual and others—should put their shoulders together to remove the present day prejudices and take the people towards the right goal of religious tolerance, brotherhood, peace and prosperity. This will help to realise the dream of our national leaders and thousands of our countrymen who devoted their life for religious tolerance, unity and freedom from time immemorial.

The message of Swami Vivekananda is most relevant today. Let us listen him when he says, "What is there to be taught more in religion than the oneness of universe and faith in one's self? All the works of mankind for thousands of years past have been towards this one goal and mankind is yet working it out. There is only one life and one world and this one life and one world is appearing to us as manifold. All the manifold is the manifestation of that *one*. That *one* is manifested himself as many, as matter, as spirit, mind, thought and everything else. It is that *one* manifesting Himself as many. Therefore, the first step for us to take is to teach the truth to ourselves and to others." It is because of this broad vision of *Vedanta*, Swami Vivekananda said Hinduism was the mother of all religions. And to prove this truth, we must go deep into the past heritage to see how religious harmony prevailed in those days.

If we are able to realise the importance of *one*, which is a divine manifestation in our own Self, that will miraculously change the attitude and outlook of our people in favour of human brotherhood and tolerance. If the Parliament of Religions has shown anything to the world it is this truth. Let us recall his last few words at Chicago: "Holiness, purity and charity are not the exclusive possessions of any church in the world and that every system has produced men and women of the most exalted characters." In the light of the message of Swami Vivekananda, let us broaden our vision and solve our socio-cultural problems amicably.

Swami Vivekananda has taught us that the greatness of Indian thought was the self-unification that gave birth to modern Hinduism. Never may we be allowed to be forgotten that on Indian soil was first heard the command from a teacher to his disciple, "Go Ye out into the all world, and preach the Gospel to every creature." It is the same thought, the same impulse of love, taking to itself a new shape, when Swami Vivekananda told the great religious philosophers of Chicago Conference, "If one religion be true, then all the others must be true. Thus the Hindu faith is yours as much as mine. And again in amplification of the same idea, we, the Hindus, do not merely tolerate, we unite ourselves with every religion praying in the mosque of the Mohammedan, worshipping before the fire of Zoroastrian and kneeling before the crucifix in the Church."

Swami Vivekananda in his speech on 26 September 1993 at Chicago said, "Upon the banner of every religion would soon be written, in spite of resistance: Help and not fight, assimilation and not destruction, Harmony and peace and not Dissension." We must follow these principles at any cost to save our people from degeneration and destruction.

On another occasion, Swami Vivekananda said, "Religion must be studied on a broader basis and not ritually. All narrow, limited fighting ideas of religion have to go. All sectarian ideas and tribal or national instincts of religion must be given up. All such ideas must be abandoned and the future religions of the world should become universal, wider than ever." Thus, the light sparking from the message of Swami Vivekananda will kill all the ills in our society and uproot the religious upheavals, purify our society and give the people a broad vision, faith, courage and wisdom to establish a truly secular India with peace and prosperity.

Summing up, the view of the great statesman of India, Sri. C. Rajagopalachari, is an eye-opener to us. "Swami Vivekananda saved Hinduism and saved India. But for him we would have lost our religion and would not have gained our freedom. May his faith, his courage and his wisdom inspire us so that we may keep safe the treasures we have received from him."

Swami Vivekananda's life was devoted to explore the great Indian cultural heritage. His life was a quest for truth, tolerance and universal understanding. His vision was true liberalism. He strongly felt that religious tolerance and understanding were indispensable to achieve peace, freedom and harmony. He believed that this goal could be achieved only through spiritual awakening and service to the poor, the oppressed and the poverty-stricken people. He advised all to serve mankind in whatever way they could to achieve the truth. His words are still powerful enough to help man to serve the suffering people: "I do not believe in a God or religion that can't wipe the widow's tears or bring a piece of bread to the orphan's mouth." He added, "The whole world has been made by the energy of man, by the power of enthusiasm, by the power of faith." He called upon his countrymen to develop muscles of iron, nerves of steel and minds like the thunderbolt, "Go all of you," he thundered, "wherever there is an outbreak of plague or famine or wherever the people are in distress, mitigate their sufferings. At the most, you may die in the attempt, what of that?"

Swami Vivekananda's mission was to spread the message of religious toleration and universal understanding. This is clear when we listen to his words, "I shall go to the mosque of the Mohammedan, I shall enter a Christian church and kneel before the crucifix, I shall enter the Buddhist temple where I shall take refuge in Buddha and in his law, I shall go into the forest and sit down in meditation with the Hindu—who is trying to see the light which enlightens the heart of every one."

We have many lessons to learn from the teachings of Swami Vivekananda. His message was for all ages. It was a message for future man. His message is still powerful enough to inspire and transform the future mankind. It aims at spiritual awakening and renaissance in society. It has immense social relevance and potential at this crucial turn of the human history, when we move into the third millennium. The spirit of Swami Vivekananda's message will help us to successfully meet the challenges of survival in the present day world.

24

Youth Power, Brain-drain and Waste of Human Energy

As we move into the 21st century, the most important topic that we should discuss and debate is youth power in the modern world. We must remember that the elders of today have an inescapable responsibility to mould each and every member of the younger generation as an intelligent and capable citizen of the future. Then only, will they be able to protect and preserve the past heritage and the present achievements for the benefit of the future man. Then only, will they be able to provide the right leadership and guidance to the people and make the future safe and secure.

It is in this light that we should recognise the importance of the youth power. At this juncture, there cannot be a topic more important than the youth and the tender population to discuss and debate. They will be builders or destroyers of the nation depending upon the way we educate, guide and mould them.

But, paradoxically, the descending youth power and the waste of human energy is a matter of serious concern to the entire world. In spite of the best support we give them, there is still waste of human energy, which no nation can afford to lose at this stage of development. It reveals that we have failed to give them proper guidance. We have not been able to develop properly their physical, mental, intellectual, moral and spiritual powers for various reasons. We have failed to develop their talents and channelise it for the benefit of mankind. This is a dangerous trend and we should reverse it through meticulous planning, and well-defined strategies to enable the nation to use the energy of the youth fully and fruitfully for national development. This trend cannot be better in other developing countries as well. There is, therefore, the need for a common strategy to cultivate, develop and use the potential of the youth for development.

Published reports indicate that about 80 per cent of the total youth population of the world is in developing countries. Surprisingly, the majority of the youth live in rural and backward areas where infrastructure facilities and guidelines for their education, training and development in the required manner are inadequate as compared to the actual requirement. Similarly, opportunities for the utilisation of their talents and energy for building up the nation and the future are very limited. Thus, the descending youth power and wasting energy and its diversion to unwanted and unproductive areas is a matter of serious concern to the whole world. Needless to say that the largescale waste of energy and power of the youth is an irreversible loss to future mankind. Some of the causes for such a state are (1) Inadequate facilities and unfavourable environment for education, self-development and growth, (2) Lack of opportunities for work, (3) Absence of proper guidance, (4) Conflict between old and new values, and (5) Modern lifestyles. So, we have to discuss the problem from a practical point of view and take corrective steps and remedial action to prevent loss of youth power and energy.

The alarming increase in the number of youngsters involved in crimes, anti-social activities and terrorism is a freightening trend. There is no doubt that it is the family and social environment and lack of opportunities that makes the youth a disappointing lot. Similarly, the large number of children and youth falling victims of drugs alcohol and other intoxicating agents indicate the deteriorating social environment in our society. According to reports, this trend is increasing at an alarming proportion and the reasons for it can be identified as lack of parental control and guidance, the weak and feeble mental structure easily susceptible to fashion-oriented lifestyles, idleness due to lack of opportunities and deteriorating living environment. Needless to say that the collossal waste of youth power and human energy is a great loss to mankind.

So, there is an urgent need to arrest and reverse this trend for the benefit of the nation and the world as a whole. There is no time to lose and we have to work together to achieve the desired results. There is also a need for well-defined policies and plans to prevent loss of youth power and human energy. We must act quickly to reverse the trend and bring back the youth to the mainstream of national life. The problem of descending youth power and wasting human energy is not the problem of an individual or family. It is not the problem of a nation alone. But it is the problem of the whole world.

Another major problem that erodes the health and power of the children and youth is pollution, health hazards and diseases. A large number of young people fall victims of various diseases and die in the prime of their life. Similarly, the death and disability among youth due to violence and accidents are also on the increase. The number of children and youth losing their mental and physical power due to malnutrition, diseases and other poor living conditions are likely to erode the future development and progress. If we are unable to take corrective steps, there will be largescale waste of productive energy in future.

It has been reported that in developing countries a large number of children are forced to work, sometimes in hazardu-ous environment. The merciless exploitation of millions of children in their age of education and development is an unhealthy practice and criminal injustice to the society. The nation is likely to lose a lot of energy of talented and educated youth as a result of child labour. The exploitation of children leads to the erosion of their physical, mental and intellectual powers and consequently their growth will be crippled or stagnated in childhood itself. When we see that the number of working children is as high as 250 million in Asia, we will be able to estimate the immeasurable loss of energy of the youth in future. The power and energy of children drained away due to lack of guidance and protection would never be regained. Their undeveloped potential goes astray as waste. If the children are utilised for work at an inappropriate age that should be termed as exploitation of immatured, half-grown and tender minds blocking their future development. This leads to disappointment and frustration.

The tender population of India, who come under the label of youth of today and tomorrow, whether in the school or college, whether employed or unemployed, whether in the urban area or rural area, should have proper access to the storehouse of new knowledge, new idea, new developments and advances. This is possible only if they are trained in the young age both at home and at school to develop a strong and disciplined mind, acquire good qualities and shape a broad outlook, and above all, a national spirit.

While discussing the youth power and energy loss, another subject of importance is brain-drain. Brain-drain and energy loss has achieved global importance in the recent times in the light of the largescale migration of young scientists, engineers, doctors and other professionals from one country to another. The most important aspect of the brain-drain is the loss of brilliant brains and human energy. However, going deep into the problem of brain-drain, we can see that there are two sides to the problem of brain-drain. The first and most important side is brain-drain from one country to another. The second and equally important is brain-drain within a country, which happens mostly due to improper utilisation of energy, lack of opportunities and facilities to work, want of appreciation and recognition of work done, and other unfavourable factors which ultimately leads to frustration leading to their migration elsewhere. Another reason for brain-drain is job prospects abroad.

Brain-drain to other countries, particularly to developed countries, is an advantage to all countries of the world as whatever development is taking place through him is moving to other parts of the world. All countries in the world can take advantage of the advances and development achieved by scientists and other professionals of a country. This is easily possible now through the globalisation channels. In this light, what the migrated scientist achieves for the benefit of mankind is more important than where he works, as the knowledge and achievements move out to other countries irrespective of the place of work.

Brain-drain within a country is very serious as it leads to waste of human energy. It happens due to lack of opportunities and employment. Hence brain-drain within a country is more important than brain-drain to other countries. This should be tackled, and energy loss prevented on an urgent basis.

Brain-drain to other countries has to be discussed in the light of the scientific and technological advantages and benefits for mankind as a whole. In other words, the technological advances, the new knowledge, the experience gained and other achievements, whether in the field of education, science, medicine, technology or other fields are shared by all countries through advancing information technology. Moreover, movement of experts, scientists, doctors, technologists professionals and other category of workers creates better understanding, friendship and cooperation among the countries. Again, the concerned country earns foreign exchange money through these migrated people. We should, therefore, evaluate the merits and demerits of brain-drain in the light of these facts. Thus brain-drain to other countries does not in any way affect the progress of a nation.

In a nutshell, when the knowledge, technology and other achievements in a country are common assets to the whole world, the persons who contributed to such achievements are also common assets in the world. It is common knowledge that, from time immemorial, experts, talented persons, scientists, technologists and other professionals moved from place to place, country to country, in search of more and more facilities and trade prospects, new knowledge and good working environment. The present status of human civilisation is the result of their achievements. As a matter of fact, they were part of the team who led and guided mankind towards progress and prosperity. Hence, brain-drain is an essential factor from the global perspective.

Our vision for the 21st century should be full and fruitful utilisation of youth power and human energy for national development. Simultaneously, we should also contribute to the overall progress and prosperity of mankind by encouraging movement of people to other countries. This strategy will help us to become partners of global progress and achievements.

25

The Spirit of the Indian Freedom Struggle—An Inspiration to Future Mankind

The spirit of India's freedom struggle is always a source of inspiration for mankind. It was a great event of the second millennium. India has shown to the world the mighty power and influence of the non-violent movement that brought freedom to the people of India and inspired several countries to win freedom.

Today, we need the spirit and basic characteristics of the freedom movement to protect the people from wars, violence, conflicts, exploitation, poverty, diseases and other calamities. The spirit of the freedom struggle is indispensable at this crucial juncture of human history to put an end to (1) fear and hatred, (2) the exploitation, atrocities and merciless killing of innocent people, and (3) the struggle for existence of the majority poor people living at the basic structure of the society. There is an imperative need to narrow down the widening gap of the socio-economic contradictions and to give the basic human rights of equality, liberty, fraternity and justice to each and every citizen. Of course, this was the true aim of our Republican freedom. This is possible only if we imbibe the spirit of the freedom struggle and follow the basic characteristics of freedom. Here, we should remember and follow the advice of Jawaharlal Nehru on our Republican freedom: "What we do with this fruit depends upon many factors, the basic factors being those on which Gandhiji laid stress throughout his career—high character, integrity of mind and purpose, a spirit of tolerance and cooperation and hard work. I can only suggest to our people that we should found our Republican Freedom on these basic characteristics and shed fear and hatred from our minds and think always of the betterment of the millions of our people."

In this light, an attempt has been made here to revive the memory of the Indian freedom movement to enable us to understand and follow the spirit and the basic characteristics of the freedom movement and rededicate ourselves for the betterment of the people.

Historians record the countrywide revolt of sepoys that took place in 1857 as the First War of Indian Independence. As a result of the exploitation, misery, suffering, injustice and slavery of the people and the general hatred and opposition to British, the uprisings of the sepoys and the associated violence spread all over India. This was known as the National Liberation Movement of 1857.

The National Liberation Movement, which involved the sepoys, the people and the kings, united the Hindus, the Muslims, the Rajputs, the Sikhs, the Brahmins and others in the army. Also it helped to unite the people of all religions, castes and races to fight against the British empire.

Although the struggle did not bring immediate results, it brought about a lot of changes in the minds of both the Indian people and the British Government. The control of Government was taken over by the British Queen by the Government of India Act of 1858. In view of the strong unity in diversity after the revolt, and also because of the strong desire of the people for freedom, the British found it difficult to continue their method of playing with the ethnic diversity of the people to achieve their goal. India lost several lakhs of patriotic and courageous people including sepoys and leaders. The struggle stirred the Indian people and laid the road for future activities.

The period between 1860 and 1884 was actually a period of change and transition after the First War of Independence. It was a period of consolidation of Indian nationalism through religious awakening, social reforms and political awareness. Development of transport and postal services together with the English language served as a common link for the movement of leaders and exchange of views and information.

During the period under review, a number of national newspapers helped to create a national awakening and consolidate Indian nationalism. These includes *Amrita Bazaar Patrika, Indian Mirror, Sanjivani and Bangalee* in Bengal, *The Hindu, Swadeshmitran, Andhra Prakasika* and *Kerala Patrika* in Madras; the *Maratta,* the *Kesari,* the *Indu Prakash* and the *Sudharak* in Bombay, *Hindustani*, the *Advocate* and *Azad* in U.P and the *Tribune* in Punjab.

During the same period, Justice Mahadev Govind Ranade, Ganesh Vasudev Joshi, S.M Chiplunkar and others organised Poona Sarvajanik Sabha in 1870 for political education which rendered yeoman service for about 30 years. In 1866, Dadabhai Naoroji founded the East India Association in London to discuss the Indian problems. The period also saw the activities of the Indian Association in Calcutta started by Anand Mohan Bose and Surendranath Banerjee in 1876 for political reforms.

Despite all these activities connected with the movement against the British, the Government was concentrating on anti-people measures such as tax imposition and rigidity of Press Act, etc. These repressive measures of the British strengthened the patriotic spirit of the people.

All these activities led to the birth of a National Movement in 1884 and the Indian National Congress in 1885. There were also a lot of isolated struggles against the British Government in different parts of the country.

NATIONAL MOVEMENT FOR FREEDOM

The national movement for saving India from the ruins of British rule was born in a meeting of 17 men of social and intellectual eminence held at Madras in December, 1884. The 17 persons who participated in the meeting were (1) Surendranath Banerjee, (2) Dadabhai Naoroji, (3) Narendranath Sen, (4) M. Ghosh, (5) S Subramania Iyer, (6) P. Rajish Naidu (7) P. Ananda Charalu (8) Vijayaranga Mudaliar (9) P. Panduranga Gopal (10) Sardar Dyal Singh (11) Harish Chandra (12) Kash Prasad, (13) Pandit Lakshminarayan (14) Charu Chandra Mittee (15) Shriram (16) K.T. Teleng (17) V. N. Mandlik.

Many of the above mentioned leaders, particularly. Surendranath Banerjee, Dadabhai Naoroji, W. C. Banarjee, K.T. Teleng, S. Subramania Iyer, Ananda Charlu and several others, who lit the flames of the new movement, carried on their historic mission through the Indian National Congress.

Several of these leaders were instrumental in organising the Indian National Congress, which was conceived by Dr. A.O. Hume. That great political movement was born at Bombay on 28 December, 1885. The fact that several of these leaders who started the National Movement in December 1884 at Madras were continuously associated with the National Congress for several years reveals, in a way, the continuity of the National Movement born in 1884 through the Indian National Congress. The history of India's freedom struggle took a different but powerful and organised turn under the dynamic Leadership of W.C. Banerjee who presided over the first meeting of the Indian National Congress.

The National Movement under the National Congress with the ultimate objective of freedom started to grow day by day and its growth echoed the problems and united voice of India at the Britsish Parliament. The multi-objective social, cultural and political, and educational movements spearheaded by

National Congress were aimed at the welfare and freedom of the Indian people.

SWADESHI MOVEMENT

The Swadeshi spirit, developed before and during the freedom struggle, had a devastating effect on the British trade income from India. It made significant contribution in building up traditional industries which in turn helped in the improvement of the industrial economy in India. Simultaneously, it also developed a patriotic spirit all over the country and gave momentum to the freedom struggle.

During the good old days of the Swadeshi Movement, handloom weaving flourished in our country. Several cotton mills were opened in Ahmedabad, Baroda and Bombay. Silk industry flourished in Assam, Bengal, Kashmir, Baroda and Mysore. As a result of the qualitative and quantitative explosion of the handloom and cotton industry, once-flourished foreign goods have become insignificant. Tata's plan to develop our own industries came during this period.

The Elders of India pointed out that the Swadeshi Movement did not mean hostility to anybody or anything but it was an awakening of an industrial patriotism in India. It brought together the masses. It exposed the talents and skill of natives. It improved the living conditions of the Indian people. The Swadeshi Movement has removed the commercial supremacy of England in India. Speaking about the splendid growth of the Swadeshi movement, Sir Vitaldas Damodar Thackersay said that all over the country today, among the young and the old, the rich and the poor, men and women, high caste and low caste, the word Swadeshi has become a household word, and the spirit of it too, we have well understood.

Speaking about the Swadeshi Movement, one of the great patriotic sons of India, Surendranath Banerjee, once appealed to the people to take the Swadeshi spirit from village to village, from town to town, district to district and spread it throughout the length and breadth of the country as part of the freedom struggle.

The heroic deeds of V. O. Chidambaram Pillai in Swadeshi Movement frightened the Government. He was an ardent champion of the freedom movement. As an agitator par excellence, he did not limit his activities to the Swadeshi propaganda alone. He created several Swadeshi institutions and became a champion of the weak and oppressed people and an enemy of the British. His activities received full support from all over India and his role was impressive in the Surat Session of the Congress. He took up the challenging task of starting a shipping service between Tuticorin and Ceylon to break the monopoly of the British Steam Navigation Company. However, on several occasions, his plan was sabotaged by the British. But his determination and patriotic spirit resulted in establishing a shipping company known as "Swadeshi Steam Navigation Company." He was arrested and imprisoned. But his heroic deeds, patriotic spirit and contribution to the Swadeshi navigation and freedom struggle are written in red letters in the history of the freedom movement.

HOME RULE MOVEMENT

On 28 April, 1916 Bal Gangadhar Tilak in Maharashtra, with headquarters at Poona, and on 15 September 1916 and Dr.Annie Besant at Madras founded the Home Rule Movement. Although the objective of both the leaders were self-government for India, Bal Gangadhar Tilak's stand was that England must fulfil its war-time promise and satisfy the demands of the Indian people immediately. Pandit Nehru supported both the leaders but worked with Annie Besant.

The Home Rule League started giving new life to the National Movement. Its objective, viz., to attain Home Rule or self-government within the British Empire by all constitutional means and to educate and organise public opinion in the country towards the attainment of the goal aimed at soon made it a popular movement all over India.

Leaders of Home Rule Movement toured throughout the country, organised meetings and processions and gave wide campaign for the Home Rule League. The result was support of the people on a massive scale. There were strikes, boycott of foreign goods and demand for social legislation. The advocates of Home Rule Movement believed in Constitutional methods and were generally opposed to violence and revolutionary agitation.

Referring to the influence of Annie Besant's work, historian C.Y. Chintamani says, "Annie Besant stirred the country by the spoken word as well as the written word, as scarcely as anyone else could do." The activities of the Home Rule League have had so deep-rooted an influence on the people that Lord Hardinge, the Viceroy, wrote to London that the agitation caused by Annie Besant and Bal Gangadhar Tilak had a distorting effect on public feelings throughout the country. After realising the growth and influence of Home Rule Movement, the British Government started repressive measures. The Press Act of 1910 was made rigid to curb propaganda, and the Defence of India Act 1915 was evoked.

JALLIANWALA BAGH TRAGEDY

On 13 April, 1919 about 20,000 people of Amritsar and nearby villages marched towards a public square protesting against the arrest of their leaders and the Rowlatt Legislation, and assembled there for a meeting. The military and police forces mercilessly shot down the unarmed crowd of thousands trapped in the square bounded on all sides with high walls/buildings. Their bullets and knives pierced through the body of patriotic

Indians leaving a thousand dead and many thousands wounded.

After the shooting at Jallianwala Bagh, General Dyer, the new master of Amritsar who had sent soldiers to kill the unarmed people, forebade the inhabitants to leave home. The physical and mental torture and the massacre that took place in all parts of Punjab were really shocking. When the suppressed news of the massacre came to light, the entire country was roused. Punjab was placed under Martial Law.

The Liberal Jurist and a Moderate, Sir P.S. Sivaswamy Aiyer's statement indicate the horrors of Punjab tragedy of 1919. It reads: The whole-scale slaughter of hundreds of unarmed men at Jallianwala Bagh without giving the crowd an opportunity to disperse, the indifference of General Dyer to the conditions of hundreds of people who were wounded in firing, the firing of machine guns into crowds who had dispersed and taken to their heels, the flogging of men in public, the order compelling thousands of students to walk 16 miles a day, the arrest and detention of 500 students and Professors, compelling school children 5 to 7 to attend on parade to salute the flag, and the invention of novel punishments like the crawling order, the skipping order and other unknown to the system of law, civil or military."

Protesting the Punjab happenings, Rabindranath Tagore renounced his "Knighthood." "The time has come", declared Rabindranath Tagore renouncing his Knighthood "when the badges of honour make our shame glaring in their congruous context of humiliation, and I, for my part, wish to stand, shorn of all special distinctions, by the side of my countrymen who for their so-called insignificance are liable to stiffer degradation not fit for human beings."

Thus the events in Punjab in 1919 created an awakening in the country opening a new chapter in the history of freedom struggle.

GANDHIJI'S NON-COOPERATION MOVEMENT

The historic resolution of non-cooperation was moved by Gandhiji in a humble but forceful voice at the Calcutta session of the Indian National Congress in September 1920. But a mere acceptance of the resolution does not end the work. Every individual has to enforce the items of resolution in so far as they apply to him.

The following was the non-cooperation resolution moved by Gandhiji:

> In view of the fact that on the Khilafat question both the Indian and Imperial Governments have signally failed in their duty towards the Musalmans of India and the Prime Minister has deliberately broken his pledged word given to them, and that it is the duty of every non-Musalman Indian in every legitimate manner to assist his brothers in his attempt to remove the religious calamity that has overtaken him, and in view of the fact that in the matter of the events of April 1919 both the said Governments have grossly neglected or failed to protect the innocent people of Punjab and Officers guilty of unsoliderly and barabarous behaviour towards them, this Congress is of the opinion that there can be no contentment in India without the redress of the two aforementioned wrongs and the only effectual means to vindicate national honour and to prevent repetition of similar wrongs in future is the establishment of Swaraj. This Congress is of the opinion that there is no course left open for the people of India but to approve and adopt the policy of progressive non-violent non-cooperation until the said wrongs are righted and Swaraj is established.

Gandhiji believed that one hundred thousand white men were able to rule three hundred and fifty million Indians only because of the cooperation from us in a thousand ways and making us more and more helpless and dependent on them. So, if we broke our cooperation by a forceful non-violent non-cooperation at all levels, that would mean freedom to India.

The Non-Cooperation Movement quickly spread to all regions of India. Gandhiji travelled a great deal throughout the country explaining the idea of non-cooperation to the masses. Nehru often accompanied him and watched how Gandhiji's popularity was growing. He witnessed everywhere Indians greeting "Let Mahatma Gandhi Win."

In Malabar, the National Movement began as early as in 1897, the year in which Sir C. Sankaran Nair was elected President of the Indian National Congress. There was widespread boycott of foreign goods. Courts and educational institutions apart from the powerful Khilafat agitation as part of the Non-co-operation Movement. The visit of Mahatma Gandhi and Maulana Shaukat Ali to Malabar area was a source of inspiration to the people to intensify their struggle.

Leaders like C. Rajagopalachari, Annie Besant and T. Prakasham also visited Kerala to provide inspiration and guidance to the movement. Great men who led the struggle in Kerala included M.P. Narayana Menon, who was sentenced to transportation of life in 1922, K.P. Kesava Menon, K. Kelappan, Muhammed Abdur Rahiman, Madhavan Nair and Moideen Koya. In Payyanur, in the northern part of Malabar, the All Kerala Political Conference met under the Presidentship of Pandit Jawaharlal Nehru and passed a resolution on complete independence.

After the unpleasant massacre of 100 devotees at Nankana Sahib and consequent upon the changes that followed, several thousands of Sikhs including many who served in the war, pledged themselves to the non-violent Non-Cooperation Movement of Gandhiji. *The Manchester Guardian* described the scene and expressed amazement. "I could not help thinking" wrote C.F. Andrews, "of the shadow of the cross. It was witness to the hold which Gandhiji had even on minds long inured to a military life."

The huge support from poor sections and women to the Swaraj Fund of Tilak at Gandhiji's behest, and the boycott of British goods on the seashore of Bombay were important events. When Yakub Khan was sent to jail for a speech at Calicut, about 70,000 people offered felicitations to him at Bombay. The entire Indian staff of Assam-Bengal Railway and all the steamship workers resorted to strike to protest against the dismissal of tea plantation workers in Bengal and they succeeded in getting the workers repatriated to homes. Having been inspired by the Non-Cooperation Movement of Gandhiji, thousands of poor peasants along the Malabar coast of South India rose against British Imperialism, landlords and moneylenders. This was known as the famous Mopala Revolt of August 1921 in Malabar. Prior to that there were several such risings in the same area.

When the Non-Cooperation Movement achieved great success in November 1921, leaders like C.R. Das, Lala Lajpat Rai, Motilal Nehru, Jawaharlal Nehru, Maulana Abdul Kalam Azad and several other leaders were arrested and sent to jail. Thus by December 1921, almost all top leaders of the movement except Gandhiji were behind bars along with an estimated 20,000 volunteers. In the beginning of 1922, the number of volunteers jailed were estimated at 30,000. This revealed the powerful impact of Non-Cooperation Movement on the British rule.

In spite of the repressive measures, came renewed vigour and pledges to fight for freedom and Swaraj. In the Ahmedabad session of Congress in December 1921, a resolution was passed proclaiming the fixed determination of the Congress to continue the campaign of non-violent non-cooperation with great vigour till the Swaraj was established. It was also decided to organise individual civil disobedience movement and mass civil disobedience movement after the people were trained in the methods of non-violence. Mahatma Gandhi was given full authority to go ahead with the programme. In February 1922, Gandhiji gave an ultimatum to the Viceroy that he would begin the mass civil disobedience if the political prisoners were not released and the repressive measures abandoned. Gandhiji decided to start the civil disobedience at Bardoli in Gujarat and a constructive programme was worked. Sardar Vallabhbhai Patel played a key role in this struggle at Bardoli.

However, the Government was not satisfied with the action of Mahatma Gandhi and the Congress. Feared of bigger troubles, Gandhiji was arrested on 13 March 1922, and was imprisoned. Gandhiji's Non-Cooperation Movement was a great success inasmuch as it awakened the whole of India for involving in the freedom struggle and shook the very foundation of the British rule in India.

Recalling the great role of Gandhiji's Non-Cooperation Movement at Rangoon in 1943, Subhas Chandra Bose said, "After the tragic events of 1919, Indians were stunned and parlysed for the time being. All the attempts for achieving liberty had been ruthlessly crushed by the British and their armed forces. Constitutional agitation, boycott of British goods, armed revolution, all had alike failed to bring freedom. There were not a ray of hope left, and the Indian people were groping in the dark for a new method and a new weapon of struggle. Just at this psychological moment, Gandhiji appeared on the scene with his novel method of Non-Cooperation or Sathyagraha or Civil Disobedience. It appeared as if he had been sent by Providence to show the path of liberty. Immediately and spontaneously the whole nation rallied round his banner. India was saved and every Indian's face was now lit up with hope and confidence. Ultimate Victory was once again assured."

SWARAJ AND NON-COOPERATION MOVEMENT

The ultimate goal of Gandhiji's Non-Cooperation Movement was achievement of Swaraj. Writing in *Young India* on 23 February 1921, Gandhiji confirmed with full confidence that if we moved forward as honest, earnest, industrious and patriotic workers for implementing our programme, then Swaraj could be established just in one year.

Swaraj means the Parliamentary Swaraj in accordance with the wishes of the Indian people. Gandhiji firmly believed that could Swaraj be achieved only through non-violent methods and the spirit of democracy and freedom could not be achieved in the midst of terrorism.

Jawaharlal Nehru firmly believed in Gandhiji's Non-Cooperation Movement. He toured along with Gandhiji throughout the country to spread the message of the movement. Inspired by the Satyagraha, Nehru once wrote, " I am an ardent believer in non-cooperation with all that it implies and I am firmly convinced that non-cooperation and no other course can bring us victory. The victory may not come in a day or in a year, but come it will and must." On 11 May 1921 when Jawaharlal Nehru went to Lucknow to see Motilal in jail, he was arrested and charged with criminal intimidation of the textile strikes. He was imprisoned and taken to Lucknow jail. On his release, he was again actively involved in the freedom struggle but was again arrested in October 1923 on a charge of conspiracy and sentenced to 30 months of imprisonment.

After the suspension of the Non-Cooperation Movement, leaders who were interested keeping up the momentum of the freedom struggle decided to continue their activities. The result was the formation of the Swaraj Party. The events after the suspension of the Non-Cooperation Movement are briefly dealt with hereunder:

C.R.Das, Motilal Nehru and other leaders evolved a new programme to enter the Legislative bodies and fight the British Government. At the Gaya session of the Indian National Congress in 1922, the Swaraj Party was formed with C.R.Das as President and Motilal Nehru as Secretary. This move was opposed by leaders like C. Rajagopalachari, Rajendra Prasad, Dr. Ansari and Vallabhabhai Patel. The party decided to remain within the Congress and fight for freedom on the new lines. The objective of the party was "uniform, continuous and consistent obstruction with a view to make the government through Legislative Assembly impossible." They also believed that constructive programmes are the only road to freedom of India.

In February 1928, the British Government appointed a Commission headed by Sir M.P. John Simon. The purpose of the Commission was to find out as to what extent India could be given independence. The objective as well as the non-inclusion of Indian members in the Commission annoyed the Indian leaders.

When the Commission arrived in Lahore, Naujawan Bharat Sabha with Bhagat Singh and others and Lala Lajpat Rai took the lead in the boycott and shouted slogans: "Simon go back", etc. Police lathi charge led to the injury of the old leader Lala Lajpat Rai resulting in his death. Mass demonstration and protests took place all over the country as part of the boycott programme. In Lucknow, Nehru led the demonstrators. Police attacks and brutalities were reported everywhere. A bomb explosion took place in the Conference Hall of the Legislative Assembly in Delhi on 8 July 1928. The events at Lucknow stirred the whole country and the Simon Commission collapsed in disgrace as reported by a historian. Bhagat Singh, Chandrasekhar Azad and Rajguru ambushed Police Officer Saunders, who inflicted injury on Lala Lajpat Rai causing his death on 'broad day-light on 17 December 1928.

The ultimatum given to the Government was to expire on 31 December 1929 and the country was preparing for an inevitable struggle. By this time, the Viceroy, Lord Irwin, announced in October-November 1929 that the goal of the Dominion status was to be met at some specified future date, and in response, Gandhiji, Annie Besant, Motilal Nehru, Jawaharlal Nehru, Sir Tej Bahadur Sapru and others signed what is known as the Delhi Manifesto, offering cooperation to evolve a scheme tor a dominion constitution suitable to India. Jawaharlal Nehru judged his action later as dangerous. It was a really amazing incident after the heroism of Bhagat Singh and self-sacrifice of Jatin Das.

CIVIL DISOBEDIENCE MOVEMENT OF 1930

The Congress at its Lahore Session in 1929 authorised the Congress Working Committee to launch the Civil Disobedience Movement. Gandhiji announced that the Swaraj would mean complete independence and a resolution to that effect was passed under the Presidentship of Pandit Jawaharlal Nehru. On December 31 1929, the flag of Indian independence was unfurled by the Congress President Jawaharlal Nehru. January 26 1930 was celebrated as the first independence day all over the country, when the people everywhere took the pledge to struggle for Poorna Swaraj. The Civil Disobedience Movement spread and by the end of 1930, Gandhiji became an indispensable force to lead the freedom struggle. He roused the dormant spirit, restored our self-respect and has provided a mighty leadership to achieving the goal of Poorna Swaraj.

Gandhiji's Civil Disobedience Movement of 1930 is an important phase of the freedom struggle. It awakened the whole nation and took the people with the movement towards the goal of complete independence. The salient features of the movement are discussed below:

The Salt Sathyagraha of 1930 under the inspiring and powerful leadership of Gandhiji was an important milestone in the history of the Indian struggle for freedom. Gandhiji informed the Viceroy that on 11 March 1930, he would begin the Satyagraha by breaking the Salt Act, and to put it in the words of a famous writer, "Gandhiji set off at the head of seventy-eight of his followers, who lived in the Ashram on the Sabarmati river in Dandi, towards the shores of the Indian ocean. The 400 km trek took three weeks. The Mahatma, by a peaceful but fearless appearance, strode at the head of an ever growing procession. People were standing along the sides of the road waving out in greeting. The peasants had earlier swilled the dusty roads with water and strewn them with flowers. The many thousand strong unarmed satyagrahis came to the shore. They prayed throughout the night of the 5th, and on the morning of April 6, 1930, and on the anniversary day of the first satyagraha of 1919, Gandhji, who incidentally never used salt himself, stepped into the water and then, coming out of the shore evaporated a symbolic pinch of salt from the sea water. This was followed by hundreds of thousands of Indians who made salt by using crude method and refused British salt."

In a meeting at Allahabad, to discuss the methods to carry on the salt satyagraha, Nehru insisted that the civil disobedience should be enlarged to cover boycott of statute and decrees of the Viceroy. He told delegates, "We should not rest content with by simply breaking the salt law, rather we should bear in mind that our aim is complete independence."

Day by day, the salt satyagraha all over the country gained momentum. The Indian National Congress moved forward successfully in the struggle. The British authorities decided to meet the situation at all costs. When massive arrests started, the Congress gave full powers to its Chairman, Jawaharlal Nehru and to the Chairman of Provisional Committees, who were really like dictators to lead the satyagraha and to name their successors. History reveals that Jawaharlal Nehru spoke day and night in March and April 1930 to awaken the people towards the goal of complete independence.

In a matter of a few months, the civil disobedience had grown so tremendously that all the old and new decrees and prohibitions issued by authorities were broken by the patriotic Indians. The result-oriented and instrumental role played by women in hundreds and thousands, participating in the March processions, satyagraha and picketing has found a significant place in the history of the freedom struggle.

The Satyagraha Movement spread throughout the country with great speed and force. Places like Bardoli and Kaira in

Gujarat, Karachi, Shiroda, Patna, Ratnagiri, Calcutta, Madras and Sholapur witnessed terrible tragedies; with the arrest of Gandhiji, the people poured into the Movement but the arrests, lathi-charge, repression and police atrocities all over India converted the non-violent and disciplined movement into political tragedies of great historical importance.

The famous salt satyagraha camp at Payyanur in Malabar made that place the 'Bardoli' of Kerala. When Gandhiji began his Dandi March in March 1930, people from different parts of the Kerala region marched to Payyanur to take part in the salt satyagraha. Although the sathyagraha camp was peaceful and successful attracting all-India attention, the police raided the camp and arrested the participants. Top leaders of Kerala who led the salt satyagraha at Payyanur included K.Kelappan, K. Madhavan Nair and Muhammed Abdur Rahiman. In a camp held at Calicut beach, P. Krishna Pillai and his co-workers displayed rare courage and heroism to defend the nation from the hands of the police.

The entire world watched the great democratic movement growing day by day under the dynamic leadership of Gandhiji, making it difficult for the British armed forces and police to deal with the situation in many places.

The will and courage exhibited by people in the satyagraha, in strikes, in processions and meetings could not be broken by lathis and bullets, particularly in Bombay, Calcutta, Peshawar and other cities. In Peshawar the Civil Disobedience Movement on 30 April 1930 resulted in an uprising of Garhwali platoons who refused to fire. They were arrested and punished by the British army. The Viceroy, Lord Irwin, was very much upset by the failure of the authorities to control the mass upsurge. He accused the entire Committee of Congressmen as illegal. He ordered intensification of arrests and street control. With the arrest of Gandhiji on 5 May 1930, almost all the leaders were in prison. But their able successors continued their struggle recording further growth of the Civil Disobedience Movement. The role played by Vinobha Bhave,

Sarojini Naidu, Abbas Tyabji, T. Prakasham, Vallabhbhai Patel and other leaders of the Congress has found an important place in the history of the Civil Disobedience Movement.

Ultimately Lord Irwin realised that a compromise discussion would alone serve the purpose and he then started work as a peacemaker and wanted the Indian National Congress to come for a Round Table Conference. After signing the terms of peace which concluded after three days talks with Gandhiji, Jawaharlal Nehru, Motilal Nehru and other leaders, the Congress Executive Committee agreed to suspend the Civil Disobedience Movement to take part in the Round Table Conference.

A settlement was signed by Gandhiji and Lord Irwin on 5 March 1931. It *inter alia,* contained the suspension of Civil Disobedience Movement, recognition of Congress as a lawful organisation, and a pledge to refrain from repressions. Nehru believed that the settlement was far from the objective of complete independence. Nehru's views on the settlement as reported in the *Hindu* dated 8 March 1931 were: "I have nothing to add to these declarations except to repeat that if we continue the negotiations, we do on the basis of the discussions at Lahore Congress and in particular with the object of securing full control by Indians of the defence services, and economic and financial policy."

In subsequent meetings, Nehru called on the patriotic Indians to consolidate the gains and strengthen unity during the interim period of truce. Nehru toured different parts of the country to tell the people to suspend the Civil Disobedience Movement for the time being.

FINAL PHASE OF THE CIVIL DISOBEDIENCE MOVEMENT

Gandhiji arrived in Bombay on 28 December 1931 after the Second Round Table Conference. During the last days of 1931 the Indian National Congress decided to start a new Civil Disobedience Movement in January 1932 but the campaign was to be limited to individual disobedience. Nehru was sentenced to two years imprisonment on 4 January 1932. Decrees giving unlimited powers to the police and courts and banning all activities of the Congress groups and other political parties were issued by the Government.

The arrest of Gandhiji and Congress President Sardar Vallabhbhai Patel on 4 January 1932 was followed by the seizing of Swaraj Bhavan on 13 January 1932. The arrests were so massive that all jails were filled up and temporary prison camps were set up in many places. There was actually police and military rule which struck a blow to the national freedom struggle. In spite of the absence of leadership caused by the arrests of all leaders, the freedom movement spread like fire and the massive involvement of women and youth added fuel to the fire.

On 8 April 1932, the day of the National Week of Remembrance of the Victims of Jallianwallah Bagh, the people of Allahabad, ignoring the threats of authorities, organised demonstrations. In the clash with the police, many people were killed and wounded. Swaruprani Nehru, widow of Motial Nehru, was among the seriously wounded. Later, she told Nehru, "I am proud to have been beaten with sticks for the cause of my motherland."

The final phase of the Civil Disobedience Movement saw widespread struggle for freedom. Spontaneous anti-feudal peasant uprising in the princely states of Jammu, Kashmir and Alwar were crushed by the troops.

On 17 August 1932 Prime Minister MacDonald announced the communal award distributing seats of the Provincial Councils on community basis. Gandhiji protested against this award and went on a fast. The Poona Pact was signed allowing the depressed classes to vote with the Hindus.

As the Third Round Table Conference ended on 24 December 1932, the British Government together with most reactionary representatives of the Indian society, passed a bill on ruling India and published it as a White Paper in February 1933. This was considered as most unsatisfactory by the leaders of the freedom movement.

The massive Civil Disobedience Movement at the beginning of the thirties had roused all levels of the Indian society to action. Strike by workers, peasant disturbances, demonstrations by traders and craftsmen, and all united upsurge of the nation, were the order of the day. Thus the anti-colonial movement in India under the dynamic leadership of Gandhiji took India near its goal of complete independence.

The Civil Disobedience Movement was suspended in May 1933 and withdrawn in May 1934 for political reasons. During the days of the satyagraha, volunteers raided salt depots in various parts of the country. Important among them were the raids of Wadala Salt Depot, Sanikkatta Salt Stores of Karnataka and the Dharsana Salt Depot. Thousands of people were beaten up and jailed for participating in the raids and satyagraha. Webb Miller, writing to the *New Freeman* newspaper, records an eyewitness account of the raid at Dharsana as under:

"In eighteen years of reporting in twenty-two countries during which I have witnessed innumerable civil disturbances, riots, streets fights and rebellions, I have never witnessed such harrowing scenes as at Dharsana. Sometimes, the scenes were so painful that I had to turn away momentarily. One surprising feature was the discipline of the volunteers. It seemed they were thoroughly imbued with Gandhi's non-violent creed."

The eyewitness account of Webb Miller only reveals the struggles and sacrifices of thousands of patriotic Indians for the freedom of India.

Describing the events of 1932, the historian, Pattabhi Sitharamayya, records:

> The Satyagrahis came forward in thousands. In 1921, they were thirty thousand in number and that was considered a big number. In 1930-31 within a short time of 10 months, ninety thousand men, women and children were convicted and sentenced. No one knows how many were beaten, but the number cannot be less than 3 or 4 times the number imprisoned. People were either beaten down into paralysis of all activity or simply tired down by a 'cat and mouse' policy. The old game of beating prisoners were renewed; office secrets were asked to be divulged, 'Where are your papers, your books, and your lists of subscriptions and volunteers? 'That was the demand of the Government and young men were harassed and unutterable things were said and unspeakable punishments were planned and executed. Imagine an advocate of the High Court being subjected to the torture of his hair plucked out one by one as a mark of police displeasure at his not giving out his name and address.

The above observation of the historian reveals the painful sufferings and sacrifices which thousands of innocent men, women and children had to undergo for aspiring relief from slavery and exploitation and for participating in the freedom struggle.

These happenings, which are in red letters in the history of our freedom movement, will have to be remembered for all times to come.

Commenting on the Civil Disobedience Movement of 1930, the famous historian and writer, Louis Fischer, said, "Gandhi did two things in 1930 : he made the British people aware that they were cruelly subjugating India and he gave Indians the conviction that they would, by lifting their heads and straightening their spines, lift the yoke from their shoulders. The British beat the Indians with batons and rifle bullets. The Indians neither cringed nor complained nor retreated. That made England powerless and India invincible."

CHANGING FACETS OF THE FREEDOM STRUGGLE

Pandit Jawaharlal Nehru's anti-colonial attitude and philosophy aimed at complete independence received full support and sympathy from Congressmen and members of the Communist Party. His call to trade unions in the Kanpur session in December 1933 to throw off the colonial yoke enraged the British leading to the arrest of Nehru and the Secretary of the State remarked "by far the most dangerous element at large in the country." In spite of the Government ban on anti-Government demonstrations, Nehru called on his fellow countrymen to celebrate 26 January as independence day. Nehru was once again arrested and sentenced to two years imprisonment on 16 February 1934 on a charge of anti-Government activities. Gandhiji called for the final and complete ending of the Civil Disobedience movement and to use constitutional methods exclusively to attain freedom.

On 4 August 1935, the Bill of the Government of India Act, 1935 was passed providing what is called a federal set-up. Jawaharlal Nehru described it as "a new charter of bondage."

The National Convention of the Congress Legislative Assembly members presided over by Pandit Jawaharlal Nehru in March 1937, called upon the Congress Parliamentary Party to put forward a demand in their respective Legislature to withdraw the Government of India Act 1935 and frame their own constitution. In 1937, Congress gained absolute majority in the Legislative Assembly in six provinces and Congressmen held ministerial posts of the Government. In the Central Legislative Assembly, Congress was led by Bhulabhai Desai and Govind Ballabh Pant was Deputy Leader. S Satyamurthy, Nilakantha Das and Asaf Ali were also active in the Central Legislative Assembly as Secretaries/Chief Whip as the case may be. But Nehru found that this had not improved the situation and the real power remained with the colonial authorities. In December 1938, at Nehru's initiative, a

National Planning Committee was set up for the economic development of the nation.

In the Haripura session of the Congress in 1938, Subhas Chandra Bose expressed full confidence in the Non-Cooperation Movement of Gandhiji, and winding up his historical address to the session, he said, “Mahatma Gandhi may be spared to our Nation for many years to come. India cannot afford to lose him, certainly not at this hour. We need him to keep our people united. We need him to keep our struggle free from bitterness and hatred. We need him for the cause of Indian independence. What is more, we need him for the cause of humanity.”

Netaji Subhas Chandra Bose, President of the Congress in January 1939, suggested that India should give an ultimatum as to when the British should give independence or all Indians must rise in a struggle against the British rule. But the leaders led by Gandhiji felt that the Indian people were not ready for such a violent struggle and a majority held this view. Nehru and several other leaders recognised the creative mind and personality, patriotism and dedication of Bose to the liberation of India. A difference of opinion as to which path—violent or non-violent—should be adopted surfaced at the Tripura session of the Congress on 10 March 1939.

In this session, a resolution put forward by Nehru was approved by a majority. It set out demands and confirmed that the fundamental aim of the Indian National Congress was to achieve complete independence for India, convening of the Constituent Assembly, elected by the people without outside interference, and approval of a democratic Constitution in the Assembly. The resolution called on all sections of the population to prepare themselves for the final battle.

QUIT INDIA STRUGGLE

The Congress Working Committee passed a resolution on 11

April 1942, rejecting the Cripps proposals. Apparently, the Cripps mission has failed. There were differences of opinion regarding the future course of action. Jawaharlal Nehru was of the view that the British Government should immediately make a formal declaration of independence. The continuous apathy of the British authorities towards India forced Gandhiji to advocate mass action to drive the British out of India. In the circumstances, Jawaharlal Nehru moved the famous 'Quit India' Resolution in the All India Congress Committee meeting at Bombay on 8 August 1942 and the resolution was passed by an overwhelming majority. This was a great event in the history of the Indian freedom struggle.

The Quit India Resolution urged immediate ending of the British Rule in India both for the sake of India and for the success of the cause of the United Nations. Addressing the delegates on the night of 8 August 1942, Gandhiji said: "I, therefore, want freedom immediately, this very night, before dawn, if it can be had. You may take it from me that I am not going to strike a bargain with the Viceory for ministries and the like. I am not going to be satisfied with anything short of complete freedom. Here is a mantra, a short one, that I give you. You may imprint it on your hearts and let every breath of you give expression to it. The mantra is 'DO or DIE'. We shall either free India or die in the attempt. We shall not live to see the perpetuation of our slavery." After the passing of the Quit India Resolution, an appeal was made to Great Britain and United Nations to respond favourably to the call of reason and justice.

But the Government reaction was repressive and cruel. All the leaders of the Congress including Mahatma Gandhi, Jawaharlal Nehru, Maulana Abul Kalam Azad, Sardar Vallabhbhai Patel, Rajendra Prasad and Acharya Kripalini were arrested on the morning of 9 Auguest 1942 in Bombay and as many as 148 leaders of the Congress were jailed on that fateful day.

The news of the arrest spread like wildfire. The entire city of Bombay was soon engulfed in commotion and agitation. There were strikes and demonstrations by all sections of the people which led to the clash between the people and the armed forces. The news quickly spread to Poona and Ahmedabad where the situation was uncontrollable. In a matter of two days, the conflagration spread to Delhi, Allahabad, Calcutta, Patna, Lucknow, Kanpur, Madras, Nagpur and several other towns and cities. The situation in Bihar and, United Province became extremely serious.

The trouble soon spread all over the country and the spontaneous reaction created patriotic fervour causing surprise to the entire world. The armed forces fired at fleeing crowds and anybody and everybody in many places. Official high-handedness was the order of the day. In the struggle, as many as 942 people died but according to Jawaharlal Nehru it was between 4,000 and 10,000. More than 60,000 people were arrested up to the end of 1942, 20,000 convicted and 18,000 detained, under the Defence of India Rules.

The Quit India Resolution indeed created a revolution in India. There were leaders like Tej Bahadur Sapru and Dr. B. R. Ambedkar who considered the resolution as ill-opportune. The British Government blamed Gandhiji for the happenings and stated that he would be released only if the Quit India resolution was withdrawn.

But Subhas Chandra Bose, the great Indian patriot and national leader, greatly appreciated the Quit India Resolution and the events thereafter. In a broadcast from somewhere in the Burma region, addressed to Mahatma Gandhi in 1943, he said, "Ever since you sponsored the independence resolution at the Lahore session of the Congress in December 1929, all members of the Indian National Congress have had one goal before them. For Indians outside India, you are the creator of the present awakening in our country. The highest esteem in which you are held by patriotic Indians outside India and by foreign friends of India's freedom increased a hundredfold when you bravely sponsored the 'Quit India' Resolution in August 1942."

A Government communication in the press on 10 February 1943 revealed that Mahatma Gandhi had undertaken a three weeks fast. It was also revealed that correspondences between Gandhiji and the Government had been going on since August 12, 1942. The correspondence were also released to the Press. The news about the fast created a stir throughout India. For many days educational institutions, business houses and shops remained closed in many parts of the country. People feared danger of life to Gandhiji in view of his weak health and advanced age, and they demanded his unconditional release from jail. An all-party meeting held at Delhi prayed for his safety and long life.

Telegrams were sent to Churchill, Stalin, Roosevelt and Marshal Chiang Kaishek for intervention and immediate release of Gandhiji. When Gandhiji's fast took a serious turn, three members of the Viceroy's Executive Council, viz., N.R. Sirkar, Homy Mody and Aney, resigned in protest against the Government's policy of detention of Gandhiji in the grave hour. A large gathering of representatives belonging to different communities met at Delhi on 19th February 1943 under the presidentship of C. Rajagopalachari.

A resolution drafted in the meeting was later passed in a Conference on 20 February, 1943 under the Chairmanship of Tej Bahadur Sapru. The resolution was forwarded to the Viceroy, and to the Prime Minister but their reply was disappointing. The Congress also urged the world leaders to intervene in the matter of Gandhiji's fast. Several provincial legislatures also demanded his unconditional release from jail.

At this time, the Government produced a 50,000 worded chargesheet making the Congress, chiefly Gandhiji, responsible for the disturbances of 1942. Gandhiji successfully completed his religious fast of 21 days and his health miraculously improved day by day. According to the attending physician Dr. B. C. Roy, an unknown power helped Gandhiji safely out of danger. However, the continued pressure from Indian leaders including Tej Bahadur Sapru, Dr. M.R. Jayakar, Dr. Sachidanand Sinha and special envoy Mr. William Phillip of President Roosevelt failed to yield results since the British Government was determined to detain Mahatma Gandhi, Nehru and other leaders till the war was over.

But the great events of 1942 and after prompted the British Government to negotiate the issue of independence with India after the war.

ROLE OF MADAME CAMA

A peep deep into the history of the freedom struggle will reveal the great contribution of Madame Cama who sacrificed her life for the freedom of India in the pre-Gandhian era. She abandoned her family life and worked with dedication for the freedom of India. She worked with Dadabhai Naoroji in London for sometime. Her activities in France created a headache to the British Government. Her journal *Vande Mataram* survived in spite of the Government ban. She and a few Indian patriots prepared a tricolour flag in 1905 and hoisted it in Berlin in the same year and in Bengal in 1907.

In the International Socialist Congress in Germany in the year 1907, she spoke, after hoisting the flag, "This flag is of Indian independence. Behold, it is born, it is already sanctified by the blood of martyred Indian youths. I call upon you gentlemen to rise and salute the flag of Indian independence."

She also assisted Veer Sarvarkar, in his activities. She published his book *The Indian War of Independence*. She tried to save Sarvarkar from British imperialism when he was arrested in London in order to implicate in what is known as the "Nasik conspiracy case." He was convicted to 50 years of imprisonment by the Bomaby High Court. The role played by Madame Cama and Veer Sarvarkar in the pre-Gandhian era has to be remembered in the freedom history of India.

INDIAN NATIONAL ARMY

The great patriotic spirit and high spirited activities of Subhas Chandra Bose always frightened the British Government who did not like his living in India. He was arrested and detained on several occasions. He was with the Indian National Congress till 1939 and he firmly believed in the Civil Disobedience Movement of Gandhiji. He was actively involved in various movements for freedom.

He always wanted India to be respected abroad and to take India to world forums for global support. After his escape from jail, he went to Germany and then to Japan and worked to achieve this objective. He was the Supreme Commander of the Indian National Army (INA) or the Azad Hind Fauj and the words 'Jai Hind' was his gift to India. Gandhiji once said, "Though, I did not accept Subhas Chandra Bose's belief in violence, I have not refrained from giving unstinted praise for his patriotism, resourcefulness and bravery."

The heroic and high spirited activities of the INA in the Far East under the dynamic leadership of Subhas Chandra Bose sent out patriotic terror to the world. The courage and determination of about 20,000 officers and men in the INA were so powerful that the mighty British army was able to hit them back only after occupying thousands of miles of India in the east. His heroic activities sent frequent shocks to the British Government. In an article Gandhiji wrote, "Bose had taught India a lesson in self-sacrifice."

Even while the INA men were marching successfully forward with the aim of reaching Delhi Red Fort to hoist the Indian flag, in a message over the radio from Burma on July 6, 1944, he sought the blessings of Gandhiji in their holy war, "I can assure you, Mahatmaji, that I and all those who are working with me regard themselves as the servants of the Indian people. The only reward that we desire for our efforts for our suffering and for our sacrifice is the freedom of our motherland. Troops of Azad Hind Fauj now fighting on the soils of India are marching ahead with all difficulties and hardships. They are pushing forward slowly but steadily. The Father of the Nation, in this holy war, for India's liberation, we ask for your blessings and good wishes—Jai Hind."

He is said to have died in an aircrash in August 1945.

Having realised the role of the INA, the Congress leaders undertook the defence of the INA officers during their trial at Delhi. For the first time after many years Nehru donned his black gown to lead the defence counsel consisting of Tej Bahadur Sapru, Bhulabhai Desai, Kailashnath and Asaf Ali. As a result of their effective defence and public demand, they were all sentenced for life instead of the original plan of death sentence and later amnestied by the Viceroy.

OTHER MOVEMENTS

The activities of Dr.B.R. Ambedkar were directly or indirectly connected with the freedom movement. As a great leader of the depressed classes, he played a notable role through satyagraha demonstrations and participation in conferences to uplift the depressed classes he represented and to take them with the freedom struggle.

Differences of opinion prevailed between Ambedkar and Gandhiji, who was himself a great reformer of the depressed classes. But Ambedkar followed the path of non-violence and satyagraha. On several occasions, he tried to minimise his differences after discussions with Gandhiji and other leaders of the Congress. The agreement on Poona Pact is an example of this. C. Rajagopalachari, Madan Mohan Malaviya, Dr. Rajendra Prasad, Dr. Solanki, Tej Bahadur Sapru and other leaders played a notable role in finalising the Poona Pact.

From 1932 onwards, he also worked for the political freedom of the depressed classes. Like Jawaharlal Nehru, he was a socialist and believer in democracy and his contribution for the constitutional development of India was significant.

The labour, peasant and underground movements during the freedom struggle had gone deep into the history of the freedom movement. The underground movements were led by Jayap Prakash Narayan, Ram Manohar Lohia and Aruna Asaf Ali. The Labour Movement in the final stages of freedom struggle were led by leaders like V.V. Giri, N.M. Joshi, N.G. Ranga and Mohanlal Saksena whose contribution both inside the Assembly and outside was significant.

FINAL STAGES OF THE FREEDOM STRUGGLE

Lord Wavell took over as the Vicroy of India. Gandhiji and a few other leaders were released from jail on 6 May 1944. Other leaders of the freedom struggle were released on 15 June 1944. Mahatma Gandhi was in touch with M.A. Jinnah to have a consensus on the Indian problem.

C. Rajagopalachari, a veteran Congress leader associated with the high command during 1921-1942 prepared a formula on the separation of Pakistan. It may be recalled that C.R was actively involved in the freedom struggle and went to jail five times. His formula envisaged appointment of a commission for demarcating Muslim-dominated areas and conducting a plebiscite of all inhabitants to decide the issue of separation. It also offered various suggestions to solve the problem. He assisted Gandhiji in his discussions with Jinnah. But there was no consensus. His formula was also not acceptable to Congress leaders.

After that another formula known as the Desai-Liaquat formula prepared by Liaquat Ali Khan, General Secretary of All India Muslim League, and Bhulabhai Desai, a Congress leader came up but failed to get recognition.

On 14 June 1946, a white paper based on the Wavell Plan embodying the Indianisation of Executive Council of the Viceroy was issued from London, and a Conference of Indian leaders was held at Simla on 25 June 1944. The Conference was a failure in the sense that it has not produced any solution to the problem.

When the Labour Party came to power in Britain on 15 August 1945, the Prime Minister of England, Clement Attlee, announced that it would help to give India a full self-Government. A month later a document was released declaring elections to the Central and Provincial Legislative Assembly. After the elections, the Constituent Assembly would be formed to prepare a new constitution for the country. However, the absence of the word independence in the declaration put leaders like Gandhi and Nehru in doubts and the declaration being vague was not helpful in achieving the goal of full independence.

By this time, the freedom movement and other connected activities got intensified. Disturbances and strikes assumed political and anti-colonial character and adopted the 'Quit India' slogan. The peasants in Punjab, Bihar and in the United Province rose against anti-peasant policies of the Government.

February 18, 1946 was a red letter day in the history of freedom struggle. Sailors of the Royal Indian Navy mutinied in Bombay which was supported by crews of ships in ports of Karachi, Madras and Calcutta. The mutineers wanted immediate end of the insults and mockery by British officers, and they hauled down British flags and hoisted the banners of the Congress and the Muslim League.

The panic-stricken Britain decided to send a Cabinet mission, consisting of Lord Pethick-Lawrence, Secretary of State for India and Burma, Sir Stafford Cripps, President of the Board of Trade, and A.V. Alexander, the first Lord of Admiralty for discussions. The Cabinet Mission arrived on 24 March 1946. A simultaneous decision to send reinforcement to India to strengthen the Indian navy was also taken.

The arrival of the Pethick-Lawrence Mission coincided with the overwhelming majority of the Congress in the Central and Provincial Legislative Assemblies after the elections in March 1946. The great victory of the Congress indicated the people's approval and whole-hearted cooperation for non-violent movement of Gandhiji.

After separate discussions with the representatives of various parties, the Pethick-Lawrence mission started negotiations on 5 May 1946 at Simla. The Congress delegation was led by Abul Kalam Azad, consisting of Jawaharlal Nehru, Vallabhbhai Patel, Abdul Ghaffar Khan and the Muslim League was represented by Jinnah and Liquat Ali Khan.

In view of the differences between the Congress and Muslim League, the latter demanding a separate Muslim State, no concrete decision was taken in the negotiations.

On 16 May 1946, the British Government, based on the report of the Mission, recommended the creation of a Union of India including British India and Princely States, which should deal with foreign affairs, defence and communication and with power to raise finance. According to the recommendation, the Indian Provinces were to be divided into three groups and each of these groups would form its own Government and work out its Constitution, and these groups would form part of the Indian Union.

The Muslim League accepted the British proposal with the remark they did not exclude the possibility of creating a Sovereign Pakistan. In the Congress, the Working Committee discussed the proposal in detail and on 7 July 1946 at the AICC session, the President, Abul Kalam Azad, called for the acceptance of the proposal. He said that the Congress had won a victory and that the independence was in sight and would be achieved without a violent and bloody uprising. He said that the British acceptance of India's demand as a result of non-violent agitation and negotiation was an unprecedented one in the world history. The session approved the proposal and elected Pandit Nehru as the new President of the Congress. Talking to a team of journalists on 10 July 1946, Nehru reportedly said that the Congress understanding of 'independence' differed radically from that of the Muslim League and the Viceroy. Independence for them was complete freedom from foreign influence and even the possibility of severing relations with the British was there. They wanted to set up an Indian Republic.

On 24 August 1946, the Indians learned the composition of the Interim Government headed by the Viceroy, Lord Wavell. Jawaharlal Nehru was given the post of Vice-Premier and Minister for Foreign and Commonwealth Affairs. Other posts were occupied by Vallabhbhai Patel, Rajendra Prasad, Sarat Chandra Bose, C. Rajagopalachari and Asaf Ali and a representative of the Scheduled Castes, Jagjivan Ram. The Indian Christians were represented by John Mathai, the Sikh by Sardar Baldev Singh, the Parsees by C.H Bhabha and the two Muslim leaders included in the Cabinet were Shafat Ahmed Khan and Ali Zaheer (not from the Muslim League). The Government took charge on 2 September 1946 and on 7 September 1946 Nehru's broadcast to the nation said: "Friends and comrades: Long Live India: Six days ago my collegues and I took up important posts in the Indian Government. A new Government has appeared in our country, an interim or temporary one as we call it, a landmark on the road to full independence. We have received many thousands of greetings and good wishes from all over the world and from all corners of India. However, we did not call on you to celebrate this historic event, we even restrained the people's enthusiasm for we want them to recognise that we are still only on the way and have yet to reach our goal. We joined this Government hoping that we would soon gain full independence, and we intend to work towards the gradual achievement of full independence of action in both our domestic and foreign policies."

The Prime Minister of England, Clement Attlee, announced on 20 February 1947 that the Cabinet intended to hand over power in India to a National Government not later than 30 June 1948. This announcement was made in the House of Commons. Lord Wavell was replaced by Lord Louis Mountbatten who arrived in Delhi on 22 March 1947 and took over charge. In September 1946, the Muslim League joined the interim Government but refused to attend the meetings called by Nehru. They appeared together with Congressmen only in the Viceroy's palace.

Gandhiji arrived in Delhi on 31 March 1947 at the invitation of the Viceroy. After discussions with Lord Mountbatten, the partition became unavoidable. On 10 May 1947 Mountbatten acquainted Nehru of his plans for the future of India at Simla. The proposal envisaged the break-up of provinces with adequate powers with a weak federal Government at the Centre. Nehru, in consultation with other Congress leaders, wrote to the Viceroy about his unacceptability of the proposals which would cut India into pieces, creating conflicts and confrontation.

After several rounds of discussions, Lord Mountbatten agreed to re-work the plan for a strong, united India. He also made preparations for the partition of the country. The Attlee Cabinet approved of the Mountbatten plan on 3 June 1947 and published a declaration. On 18 July 1947 the British Parliament passed the Indian Independence Act. The Act envisaged division of India into Hindustan and Pakistan. At the instance of Lord Mountbattern, the British Government decided to advance the date of handing over of power from June 1948 to 15 August 1947.

FLAMES OF FREEDOM

The late evening of 14 August 1947 saw a festively illuminated Delhi packed with thousands of our countrymen anxiously waiting to witness the first session of the Constituent Assembly. Around midnight, the President of the Assembly, Dr. Babu Rajendra Prasad, announced a new State, the Union of India, and in that solemn moment the transfer of power took place. They paid tributes to the thousands of known and unknown countrymen who had sacrificed their lives for the freedom of India.

In that great moment of historic transition, the emotion-charged speech of Pandit Jawaharlal Nehru awakened the world. The speech delivered by him in the Constituent Assembly on the eve of independence on 14 August 1947 as follows:

> "Long years ago we made a tryst with destiny, and now the time comes when we shall redeem our pledge, not wholly or in full measure, but very substantially. At the stroke of the midnight hour, when the world sleeps, India will awake to life and freedom. A moment comes, which comes but rarely in history, when we step out from the old to the new, when an age ends, and when the soul of a nation, long suppressed, finds utterance. It is fitting that at this solemn moment we take the pledge of dedication to the service of India and her people and to the still larger cause of humanity.
>
> At the dawn of history, India started on her unending quest, and trackless centuries are filled with her striving and the grandeur of her success and her failures. Through good and ill fortune alike she has never lost sight of that quest or forgotten the ideals which gave her strength—we end today a period of ill fortune and India discovers herself again. The achievement we celebrate today is but a step, an opening of opportunity to the greater triumphs and achievements that await us. Are we brave enough and wise enough to grasp this opportunity and accept the challenge of the future?
>
> Freedom and power bring responsibility. The responsibility rests upon this Assembly, a sovereign body representing the sovereign people of India. Before the birth of freedom we have endured all the pains of labour and our hearts are heavy with the memory of this sorrow. Some of' those pains continue even now. Nevertheless, the past is over and it is the future that beckons to us now.
>
> That future is not one of ease or resting but of incessant striving so that we may fulfil the pledges we have so often taken and the one we shall take today. The service of India means the service of the millions who suffer. It means the ending of poverty and ignorance and disease and inequality of opportunity. The ambition of the

> greatest man of our generation has been to wipe every tear from every eye. That may be beyond us, but as long as there are tears and suffering so long our work will not be over.
>
> And so we have to labour and, to work, and work hard to give reality to our dreams. Those dreams are for India, but they are also for the world, for all the nations and peoples are too closely knit together today for anyone of them to imagine that it can live apart. Peace has been said to be indivisible; so is freedom, so is prosperity now, and so also is disaster in this one world that can no longer be split into isolated fragments.
>
> To the people of India, whose representatives we are, we make an appeal to join us with faith and confidence in this great adventure. This is no time for petty and destructive criticism, no time for ill will or blaming others. We have to build the noble mansion of free India where all her children may dwell."

At about 4'o clock in the evening on 15 August 1947, in the jam packed Red Fort of Delhi, in the presence of leaders and Indian people, Pandit Jawaharlal Nehru, the first Prime Minister of India, hoisted the flag of free India.

And in that great moment, Mahatma Gandhi, the Father of the Nation, was away in Calcutta observing fast, and spinning to mark the independence day. An unending stream of people wended their way to his residence and offered their respects to him.

In that great hour, the dreams of great leaders of the freedom struggle like Nana Sahib, Rani Lakshmi Bhai, Tantia Tope, Bahadur Shah, Begum Hazrat Mahal, Lokkamanya Tilak, Dadabhai Naoroji, Chandrasekar Azad, Ashfaqallah, Bawa Khara Singh, Madam Cama, Subhas Chandra Bose, Abul Kalam Azad, Govind Ballabh Pant, Rafi Ahmed Kidwai and many other Indians came true.

The flames of freedom brought glory to the national leaders from Bakim Chandra Chatterjee who galvanised a supine nation through his Vande Mataram to Pandit Jawaharlal Nehru who spoke so much and fought so long to keep our tryst with destiny. The flames of freedom stood as a symbol of the 27-year-long non-violent struggle led by Mahatma Gandhi, who took over the responsibility in 1919, in an environment of despair and failure, with a pledge to free India from slavery and exploitation. And in that great struggle, Gandhiji welded the entire populace into an integrated nation with pride in its heritage and confidence in its future and led them towards the goal of freedom. Gandhiji ultimately proved that the spirit of non-violence is mighter than the sword and taught a great lesson to the world.

Soul-stirring scenes of national rejoicing marked by a unique demonstration of Hindu-Muslim unity were witnessed during the independence day celebrations. Vast crowds of Hindus, Muslims and other categories of people freely mingled with each other with joy and happiness to celebrate the occasion. The fraternisation that began during-the first war of independence in 1857 once again confirmed the unity and integrity of India.

And for the Iron Man of India, Sardar Vallabhbhai Patel who stood with Gandhiji during the trials and tribulations of the freedom struggle, and who united the princerely states and made India a strong nation, said on the eve of independence, "Let us not forget in the joy of the hour the stupendous responsibilities and obligations which freedom has brought in its wake."

NEW MILLENNIUM MESSAGE

The message contained in the historic speech of Pandit Jawaharlal Nehru truly reflects the spirit of the Indian freedom struggle. It is an inspiring message for generations to come. It is as relevant today as it was in 1947. If we are prepared to imbibe the spirit of that message on the eve of the new millennium and work together with total dedication, we can no doubt solve our problems and live with peace. That way, we can make a great India, where the democratic rights of equality, liberty, justice and fraternity will come true in the life of each and every citizen. Needless to say, the spirit of the Indian freedom struggle is a source of inspiration for future mankind to establish a world without fear and without hunger; and ultimately a society with peace and prosperity everywhere.

Bibliography

Abul Kalâm Azad, *India Wins Freedom* (1959).

Agarwal L.N., *Indian National Movement.*

Ahulwalia, M.M., *Freedom Structure in India* (1858-1909).

Aurobindo Ghose, *The Renaissance in India* (1920).

Bal Gangadhar Tilak, *Speeches and Writings.*

Balan K, *Education, National Integration and Development*, Ashish Publishing House, 1990.

Bipin Chanara Tripathi and Barun, D.C., *Freedom Struggle* (1972).

Chatterjee, A.C., *India's Structure for Freedom* (1947).

Chintamani, C.Y., *Indian Politics since the Mutiny* (1940).

Convocation Addresses of ANNA, Prof. A. K. Moorthy, Ed. Anna Publishing House, Chennai.

Dhananjan Keer, *Dr. Ambedkar-Life and Mission.*

Frolov, *Global Problems and the Future of Mankind*, 1982, Progress Publishers, Moscow.

Gandhi, M.K., *Collected Works* (1968).

Gandhi, M.K., *Speeches and Writings.*

Gandhi, M.K., *Swaraj.*

Hoyland, J.S., *Gopalakrishna Gokhale—His Life and Speeches* (1930).

Human Development Report 1998, UNDP.

Human Development Report 2000, UNDP.

Humanscape, Vol VII, Issue VIII, August 2000, Mumbai.

Jawaharlal Nehru, *Autobiography.*

Jawaharlal Nehru's Speeches (1946-1949), Publication Division New Delhi.

Jayat S. Bright (Ed.), *Important Speeches and Writings of Subhas Chandra Bose* (1946).

Kashyap, Subash C., Citizens and the Constitution, 1997 Publication Division, New Delhi.

Mazumdar, R.C., *History of Freedom Movement in India.*

Mukherjee, Hirendranath, *India's struggle for Freedom—A history* (1946).

Nemai Sadhan Bose, *The Indian National Movement* (1965).

Newsletter, April-June, 2000, American Information Resource Centre, Chennai.

Pattabhi Sitharamayya, *History of Indian National Congress* (1885-1935).

Peter, F, Drucker, Managing in Turbulent Times.

________________, *Productivity in the Age of Technology,* Centre for Public Sector Studies, New Delhi.

Roman Rolland, *Mahatma Gandhi* (1924).

Smith, Vincent, A., *Oxford History of India.*

Statistical Outline of India—1998-99, Tata Services Ltd, Mumbai.

Tarachand, *History of Freedom Movement in India, Vol. I, II & III.*

The Complete Works of Swami Vivekananda, Advaita Ashrama, Mayavati Himalayas, (1986)

The New Sunday Express dated 27.5.2001.

The Indian Express, Dt. 11-9-98.

The State of the World's Children, 2000-UNICEF.

The Universal Text Book of Religion and Morals, Part I, 1962 Annie Besant, The Theosophical Publishing House, Madras.

Women and the Constitution, 1997, Indian Social Institute, New Delhi.

World Health Report 1999, World Health Organisation.

Yuva Bharathi, August 1973, Chennai.

Index